AMANDINE GARDE AND
GREGORY MESSENGER

PUBLIC HEALTH AND INTERNATIONAL ECONOMIC LAW

Preventing Non-Communicable Diseases
and Promoting Better Health for All

BRISTOL
UNIVERSITY
PRESS

First published in Great Britain in 2025 by

Bristol University Press
University of Bristol
1-9 Old Park Hill
Bristol
BS2 8BB
UK
t: +44 (0)117 374 6645
e: bup-info@bristol.ac.uk

Details of international sales and distribution partners are available at bristoluniversitypress.co.uk

British Library Cataloguing in Publication Data
A catalogue record for this book is available from the British Library

ISBN 978-1-5292-4276-8 paperback
ISBN 978-1-5292-4277-5 ePub
ISBN 978-1-5292-4278-2 ePdf

Cover design: Blu inc
Front cover image: Stocksy/Javier Pardina

Contents

List of Figures and Tables

List of Abbreviations

BIT   bilateral investment treaty
FCTC   Framework Convention on Tobacco Control
FDI   foreign direct investment
FET   fair and equitable treatment
FoPNL   front-of-pack nutrition labelling
FTA   free trade agreement
GATT   General Agreement on Tariffs and Trade
GATS   General Agreement on Trade in Services
IIA   international investment agreement
IP   intellectual property
ISDS   investor-state dispute settlement
MFN   most-favoured nation
MNC   multinational corporation
NCD   non–communicable disease
TBT   technical barriers to trade
TRIPS   Trade-Related Aspects of Intellectual Property Rights
WHO   World Health Organization
WTO   World Trade Organization

Acknowledgements

This book originates from an idea we first discussed in 2017. As we reflected on our policy experience, working for over a decade with policy actors interested in trade, health, or trade and health policy, we noted that in the area of our collective academic expertise – across international trade, public health, consumer protection, and non-communicable disease (NCD) prevention law and policy, there was no book sufficiently tailored to the needs of policy actors to clearly and succinctly analyse the relationship between international economic law and public health – and the prevention of NCDs more specifically. This book is the product of our efforts to fill this gap.

As we have worked on this book, we have benefited from the support of a number of colleagues.

First, Grace Carroll and her colleagues at Bristol University Press have been a genuine pleasure to work with. Grace embraced the project from the outset and supported us throughout with kindness and helpful advice. We were attracted to Bristol University Press' Policy and Practice series, which allows academic analysis to be presented in a relatively short format intended for both academic and policy audiences. We benefited from Bristol University Press' expertise in this area. As part of this process, we received extremely useful comments from the colleagues who reviewed both our proposal and the draft we submitted. These reviewers worked anonymously, as is often the case, and while we are unable to name them, we thank them very warmly for their generous and thorough engagement with our work. We would also like to thank our colleagues at Liverpool and Bristol for accepting to review the submitted manuscript to ensure the accuracy of our legal analysis: Dr Christian Delev, Professor Mavluda Sattorova, and Dr Sujitha Subramanian. The responsibility for any mistakes that may remain is nonetheless entirely our own.

Before contacting Bristol University Press, we developed the book proposal and the rough draft that provided the basis of the work with funding we received from the UK Prevention Research Partnership (UKPRP)-funded Prevention of Non-Communicable Disease Using Trade Agreements (PETRA) network. We would specifically like to thank Heather Lodge, who has been the driving force behind this network from its inception in 2018 to the moment it concluded its activities in 2023. We would also like to thank two PETRA co-investigators: Professors Mzwandile Mabhala and Paul Lincoln, who strongly supported the project and now sit on the Advisory Board of the related National Institute for Health and Care Research (NIHR) project that we co-lead on Navigating Trade Challenges at the WTO Technical Barriers to Trade Committee to Prevent Non-Communicable Diseases to Promote Better Health for All.[1]

We are delighted to be working directly on this NIHR project with Marcelo Campbell, Professor Gabriel Siles-Brugge, and Dr May van Schalkwyk. Rarely has work been such a joy: for all the happy moments that we have spent together with these three great colleagues, also working on the commercial determinants of health, lobbying and legal strategies, and the trade and health nexus, we shall be forever grateful. We acknowledge the significant support we have received from the NIHR not only for funding this ongoing

[1] NIHR (NIHR204663). The views expressed are those of the author(s) and not necessarily those of the NIHR or the Department of Health and Social Care.

project (2023–2026), but also for enabling us to publish this book in open access to ensure that it is disseminated far more widely than academic books tend to be.

This book, we hope, presents a useful systematization and novel analysis of the relationship between international trade and investment law, on the one hand, and the prevention of NCDs, on the other hand. It is published at a time when this relationship is increasingly becoming the focus of combined academic and policy efforts. We look forward to pursuing our work through the different initiatives and collaborations in which we are involved, not only the NIHR project we have already mentioned, but also the Trade & Public Policy (TaPP) Network which, in three years of existence, has become the largest network of academic experts on UK trade policy and the Law & Non-Communicable Diseases Research Unit, which has, for the past ten years, contributed to building the legal capacity of public health actors around the world to adopt and implement effective NCD prevention laws and policies. Plenty of work remains to be done to promote healthier environments, and we hope that this book can support this important work.

We are grateful to all the colleagues we have worked with and the policy actors around the world for whom we have provided training courses over the years. They are too many to name, but they will know who they are. We also thank the students that we have taught and have provided a very useful sounding board over the years, particularly those who took the LLM in International Trade Law and Public Health at the University of Liverpool that we developed a few years ago.

Last but not least, we are very grateful to each other for the mutual support and hours of work spent together in such good spirits. We hope that through this close collaboration and friendship, this book has achieved its objective of being more than the sum of its parts.

This book represents the law as of 1 December 2024.

ONE

Introducing Non-Communicable Diseases and the Trade in Tobacco, Alcohol, and Unhealthy Food

1.1 Introduction

Non-communicable diseases (NCDs), also known as chronic diseases, kill 41 million people each year, equivalent to 74 per cent of all deaths globally. Cardiovascular diseases account for most NCD deaths, followed by cancers, chronic respiratory diseases, and diabetes. Together, these four groups of diseases account for over 80 per cent of all premature NCD deaths.[1]

The past two decades have seen a dramatic increase in awareness and understanding of the factors contributing to the growing prevalence of NCDs. However, while the actions needed to prevent them are better understood, this has not always translated into effective policy interventions.

There is growing interest in addressing the determinants of health, especially those shaped by the practices of economic actors (known as the commercial determinants of health) and

---

[1] WHO, 'Noncommunicable Diseases': https://www.who.int/health-top ics/noncommunicable-diseases

their implication for growing rates of NCDs. The focus has principally been on the tobacco, alcohol, and food industries. This is especially relevant as governments have sought to move away from NCD prevention models based on public-private partnerships to those based on the adoption of legally binding rules. Setting formal parameters within which industries associated with ill health can operate has been met with fierce resistance from these industries, and particularly large multinational corporations (MNCs) and their allies. Beyond the range of lobbying activities underpinning such resistance, MNCs have mounted – or have threatened to mount – legal challenges at national and international levels, including those anchored in international economic law, and two of its key branches more specifically: international trade law and international investment law.[2]

As a field of public international law, international economic law constitutes part of the legal regime that governs the conduct of states and international organizations in international economic relations. It is significant, as international trade and investment law influences what governments can or cannot do when pursuing NCD prevention policies. It can also empower private actors to challenge these policies.[3]

This book sheds light on the international economic law implications for the regulation of the tobacco, alcohol, and food industries. After summarizing the health challenge at stake – the prevention of NCDs, highlighting the implications of tobacco, alcohol and unhealthy food consumption in the

---

[2] The Selected Bibliography provides a selection of introductory texts on each of these fields of law.

[3] This is a dynamic to which we will return throughout the book. It is often noted within the public health community and civil society more broadly through terms such as 'regulatory chill', referring to the ability of private actors to discourage the introduction of public health regulation in the shadow of legal obligations. See Chapter 3, section 3.3 and Chapter 8, section 8.2.

growing prevalence of NCDs (section 1.2), this introductory chapter focuses on the legal strategies industry actors, and primarily large MNCs, have used to avoid government regulation, to limit its scope and therefore its impact on their operations, or to delay its implementation (section 1.3). We then introduce the importance for the public health community of understanding international trade and investment law to effectively counter the opposition that industry actors have mounted – or could mount – against the adoption and implementation of government-led measures regulating industry actors associated with ill health, particularly those involved in the manufacture, distribution, and marketing of tobacco, alcohol and unhealthy food (section 1.4). This chapter then identifies other key actors involved when considering the trade/investment and health nexus (section 1.5), before presenting the approach taken in the remaining chapters, setting the scene for the remaining analysis and aims in the book (section 1.6).

1.2 The prevention of NCDs as a major public health challenge

The human and economic cost of NCDs is immense: it affects the health of individuals, increases the cost to national health services, and entails broader societal costs such as lost productivity, absenteeism, and increased health inequities.[4] The rapid growth of NCDs also threatens sustainable development, as their burden continues to rise disproportionately in developing countries.

---

[4] The WHO defines health inequities as 'systematic differences in the health status of different population groups'. They arise from social conditions in which people are born, grow, live, work, and age. Health equity is achieved when everyone can attain their full potential for health and wellbeing: https://www.who.int/news-room/facts-in-pictures/detail/health-inequities-and-their-causes

The recent COVID-19 pandemic has further aggravated the situation in many countries, as people living with NCDs are at greater risk of severe illness and death due to COVID-19. More generally, there are close and increasingly documented connections between the many existential health challenges we face today, including NCDs, infectious diseases, environmental degradation, and the climate crisis.[5]

NCDs are largely preventable, and a clear international consensus has emerged over the past 15 years that, through the adoption of coordinated, evidence-based prevention strategies, governments – working individually and collectively at the local, national, regional and global levels – can reverse the growing prevalence of NCDs around the world. In particular, the effective prevention of NCDs requires that governments address their main underlying risk factors: unhealthy diets, physical inactivity, and tobacco and alcohol use (to which the World Health Organization [WHO] has more recently added air pollution). Evidence has accumulated regarding what states should do to make our living environments healthier, fairer, and more sustainable. Specifically, the WHO Global Action Plan for the prevention and control of NCDs has identified a suite of policies including the imposition of information schemes (for example, product labelling), pricing policies (for example, excise taxes), marketing restrictions, and product reformulation. These policies are particularly worth considering as they offer a good financial return on investment, demonstrating that that preventing NCDs makes social and economic sense.

The imperative to address the burden of NCDs is reinforced by the growing recognition that NCDs should also be envisaged as a human rights concern. Individuals hold a range of human

---

5   See, in particular, B Swinburn et al, 'The Global Syndemic of Obesity, Undernutrition, and Climate Change: The Lancet Commission Report' (2019) 393 *The Lancet* 791.

rights, not least the right to the enjoyment of the highest attainable standard of health, but also the right to adequate nutritious food, the right to life, the right of the child to have their bests interests upheld as a primary consideration in all policies concerning them, which states have a duty to respect, protect, and fulfil.[6]

Law holds the potential to contribute to the transformation of our living environments. This is particularly so if it is supplemented by evidence-based, government-led, public health education campaigns and other appropriate policy tools. This is why law should be seen as paramount in a government's response to the growing burden of NCDs.

The transformation of our living environments: reducing consumer demand for harmful commodities through the multifaceted regulation of the tobacco, alcohol, and food industries

- Provision of consumer information (disclosure requirements, regulation of claims, front-of-pack labelling, warnings and so on).
- Provision of consumer education (for example, via school curricula).
- Regulation of public procurement (provision of food in school canteens, hospitals, prisons and so on).
- Imposition of marketing restrictions (for example, on tobacco products, alcoholic beverages, unhealthy food, including non-alcoholic beverages, energy drinks, and infant food).
- Use of economic instruments (for example, taxation and minimum unit pricing on tobacco, alcohol and unhealthy food, and subsidies and tax reduction on healthy food).
- Product reformulation (for example, trans fat elimination and alcohol/salt/sugar/fat content reduction).

---

[6] On human rights and NCD prevention, see the literature discussed in ME Gipsen and B Toebes (eds), *Human Rights and Tobacco Control* (Cheltenham: Edward Elgar, 2020) and A Garde, J Curtis and O De Schutter (eds), *Ending Childhood Obesity: A Challenge at the Crossroads of International Economic and Human Rights Law* (Cheltenham: Edward Elgar, 2020).

- Limiting product size and multi-buy offers (for example, on alcohol or food).
- Licensing and planning regulation (for example, no fast-food takeaways near schools).
- Imposition of age limits (for example, on the sale of tobacco/ alcohol/energy drinks).

Several (though not all) of these regulatory interventions are listed in the WHO 'best buys',[7] and many of them have international trade and investment law implications, as will be discussed throughout this book. Many of them have also been tried and tested in different parts of the world, although they will have been adapted to local circumstances. Their effectiveness should be regularly monitored and evaluated to ensure that they do indeed contribute to the prevention of NCDs.

In spite of the evidence supporting legal interventions, states around the world have often failed to adopt and implement the laws and regulations necessary to minimize the impact of the main NCD risk factors, despite their explicit commitment 'to act in unity to create a just and prosperous world where all people can exercise their rights and have equal opportunities to live healthy lives in a world free of the avoidable burden of [NCDs]'.[8]

1.3 The commercial determinants of health and their implications in growing rates of NCDs: the harmful health impact of tobacco, alcohol, and food MNCs

In recent years, evidence has led to a move away from personal responsibility to biomedical discourses that recognize the structural factors that contribute to ill health and their

---

[7]   WHO, *Tackling NCDs: Best Buys and Other Recommended Interventions for the Prevention and Control of Noncommunicable Diseases* (Geneva: WHO, 2nd edn, 2024).

[8]   Resolution 73/2, para 49.

complex interactions. This complexity is increasingly well documented and it has become clear that the commercial determinants of health are largely implicated in the growth of NCDs worldwide, to the extent that some of their products and commercial practices drive ill health and increase associated health inequities.[9]

The concept of commercial determinants of health contrasts with a more traditional understanding of health determinants, which have predominantly focused on factors such as individual behaviours and healthcare services based on a largely biomedical understanding of health. The commercial determinants of health and the evidence underpinning this field call for a redefinition of what or who is seen as a driver of harm, and therefore the types of policies and practices needed to promote and protect public health.[10]

The commercial determinants of health are varied and so is their contribution to ill health. As such, they are difficult to classify. In this book, we focus primarily on tobacco, alcohol, and food MNCs and their allies, often referred collectively as 'Big Tobacco', 'Big Alcohol', and 'Big Food'. The rationale for such a focus stems from the fact that these MNCs are powerful actors that have the capacity to operate across borders in several jurisdictions and are therefore best placed to rely on international trade and investment law as part of their multifaceted corporate strategies, having the resources required

---

[9] The 2023 Lancet Series defines the commercial determinants of health as 'the systems, practices and pathways through which commercial actors drive human health and health equity': AB Gilmore et al, 'Defining and Conceptualising the Commercial Determinants of Health', *The Lancet*, 401 (2023) 1194.

[10] M van Schalkwyk et al, 'Back to Our Roots or Sowing New Seeds: Thinking Anew on the Paradigms of Health, Harm and Disease', *Journal of Public Health* (2022) 44(Supplement_1): i28–i33; and S Friel et al, Commercial determinants of health: future directions', *The Lancet* 401 (2023) 1229.

to challenge governments. That said, many of the principles we discuss throughout this book similarly applies to other commercial determinants of health, including the fossil fuel, pesticide, genetically modified organism (GMO), gambling, vaping, and firearms industries.[11]

Large tobacco, alcohol, and food MNCs often disproportionately affect countries and populations that are not profiting directly from trade in their products, services, and brands. Instead, these countries are left facing the burdens of these harms. MNCs therefore contribute to health inequities, both within and between countries.[12] They also affect other factors associated with ill health and health inequities through broader economic systems and economic determinants, including economic development or trade policies, social, economic, and political systems, and finance or investment flows.[13] Countries with commodity-dependent economies are especially vulnerable, such as small island developing states and least developed countries that often face greater pressure from MNCs with significant market power.[14]

The tobacco, alcohol, and food industries are highly concentrated. States may therefore have to deal with MNCs that have vast resources and influence. This economic power both stems from and increases the ability of these industries to

---

[11] For a discussion apprehending the commercial determinants of health broadly (beyond the Lancet Series mentioned earlier), see N Maani, M Petticrew and S Galea (eds), *The Commercial Determinants of Health* (Oxford: Oxford University Press, 2022).

[12] For a succinct expose of the relationship between the commercial determinants of health and health inequities, see: https://www.who.int/news-room/fact-sheets/detail/commercial-determinants-of-health

[13] This is well demonstrated by the Lancet Breastfeeding Series, and in particular P Baker et al, 'The Political Economy of Infant and Young Child Feeding: Confronting Corporate Power, Overcoming Structural Barriers, and Accelerating Progress', *The Lancet* 401 (2023) 503.

[14] WHO, *Noncommunicable Diseases and Mental Health in Small Island Developing States* (Geneva: WHO, 2023).

operate at all levels, from the very local to the global, and to benefit significantly from the opportunities that globalization and economic liberalization offer. Economic liberalization in particular has increased foreign direct investment (FDI) in the tobacco, alcohol, and food industries. However, there is growing evidence that such liberalization has negatively affected public health by promoting the trade and, indirectly, the consumption of commodities implicated in growing rates of NCDs worldwide.[15]

The WHO 'best buys' focusing on the prevention of NCDs call for the regulation of the tobacco, alcohol, and food industries, including MNCs. Nevertheless, regulating these industries effectively has proven challenging and, overall, the measures that states have adopted have not been commensurate to the challenges that NCDs pose. Progress towards the objectives set to reduce NCD prevalence remains insufficient:

> *Enhanced* political leadership to advance strategic, outcome-oriented action across and policy coherence for the prevention and control of NCDs, in line with whole-of-government and health-in-all policies approaches … The world has yet to fulfil its promise of implementing, at all levels, measures to reduce the risk of premature death and disability from [NCDs].[16]

The next section reflects on why political will has been lacking, looking specifically at the challenges that these industries have

---

[15] See the extensive literature review conducted by Milsom et al focusing specifically on corporate influence on trade regimes as a barrier to policy action on NCDs: P Milsom et al, 'Corporate Power and the International Trade Regime Preventing Progressive Policy Action on Non-Communicable Diseases: A Realist Review', *Health Policy and Planning* 36(4) (2021) 493.

[16] UN General Assembly Resolution 73/2, September 2018, at paras 3 and 4 (emphasis added).

mounted – both formally and informally – against regulation by using international trade and investment agreements as part of their legal strategies.

1.4 From the adoption of self-regulatory pledges to legal challenges anchored in international trade and investment law

The tobacco, alcohol, and food industries have long claimed that they are 'part of the solution' and should be trusted by governments to regulate themselves. They have also used their economic power to challenge governments that *have* attempted to regulate their commercial practices or increase the price of their goods or services or restricted the use of their brands. As evidence that self-regulation does not work has accumulated, the international community has increasingly called on states to regulate, and to do so as comprehensively as possible in order to limit investment shifts from regulated to unregulated practices, and therefore ensure the effectiveness of NCD prevention policies.[17]

It is noteworthy that the more robust the NCD prevention policies, the more likely it is that industry actors will challenge them in court. These challenges are raised before various courts and tribunals that operate at national (domestic courts), regional (for example, the Court of Justice of the European Union or the European Court of Human Rights in Europe), and international levels (for example, an investment tribunal or WTO panels).

Moreover, challenges often rest on a wide range of legal arguments, drawing on different subdisciplines of law, of

---

[17] This point is discussed more extensively in A Garde, J Curtis and O De Schutter, 'Ending Childhood Obesity: Introducing the Issues and the Legal Challenge', in A Garde, J Curtis and O De Schutter, *Ending Childhood Obesity: A Challenge at the Crossroads of International Economic and Human Rights Law* (Cheltenham: Edward Elgar, 2020).

which international economic law is an important one, but not the only one. Tobacco, alcohol, and food MNCs have invoked domestic constitutional or human rights law (for example, when arguing that an advertising or labelling measure infringes the right to free – commercial – expression or the right to – intellectual – property [IP]). They have also used domestic administrative law (for example, in a judicial review claiming that an authority does not have the powers to regulate). Challenges may also be based on the compatibility of domestic law with regional (for example, the law of the European Union [EU] or the law of the Council of Europe) or international human rights law (for example, the law as enshrined in an international human rights or global health convention, such as the Framework Convention on Tobacco Control or FCTC).[18] Challenges may also rest on the failure of a government to comply with international economic law, including international trade law and international investment law, as will be discussed throughout this book. The point here is that the *combination* of these challenges to NCD prevention measures requires governments to anticipate the variety of possible legal arguments that could be made in order to be in a position to respond to each and every one of them as effectively as possible. This applies during their development, during their adoption, and after their implementation, to ensure that the measures are not *successfully* challenged.

To bring the point home more practically, Table 1.1 illustrates the range of challenges that a government could face when adopting laws and regulations intended to standardize product

---

[18] On the FCTC, see in particular A Taylor, 'Governing the Globalization of Public Health', *Journal of Law, Medicine & Ethics* 32 (2004) 500; A Taylor and A McCarthy, 'Human Rights in the origins of the FCTC', in ME Gispen and B Toebes (eds), *Human Rights and Tobacco Control* (Cheltenham: Edward Elgar, 2020); and M Melillo, *Weaponising Evidence: A History of Tobacco Control in International Law* (Cambridge: Cambridge University Press, 2024).

Table 1.1: Challenging tobacco packaging regulation

Domestic legal systems
• Claims challenging tobacco plain packaging (TPP) in national courts, including constitutional courts
• Raised directly by companies and/or industry groups[19]
Free Trade Agreements (FTAs) and other regional economic integration regimes
• Claims based on commitments to liberalize and integrate markets within specific regions
• Raised by companies directly or by governments[20]
International investment regime
• Claims based on commitments under international investment agreements to protect companies from unfair treatment, or to limit the enjoyment of their property (including IP)
• Raised directly by companies against regulating governments through a process of legal arbitration ('Investor-State Dispute Settlement')[21]
International trade regime
• Claims challenging TPP based on duties on states to regulate in certain ways, and protect IP
• Raised by WTO Members, lobbied by companies and/or industry bodies[22]

---

[19] For example, decision of the British Court of Appeal in *R (British American Tobacco & Others) v Secretary of State for Health* [2016] EWCA Civ 1182.

[20] For example, Judgments of 4 May 2016 in Cases C-358/14 *Poland v Parliament and Council*, C-477/14 *Pillbox 38 (UK) Limited v Secretary of State for Health* and C-547/14 *Philip Morris Brands SARL and Others v Secretary of State for Health*.

[21] For example, *Philip Morris v Uruguay* (2016) ICSID N° ARB/10/7.

[22] For example, *Australia – Tobacco Plain Packaging* (DS434, DS435, DS441, DS458, DS467).

packaging. We have chosen the example of tobacco packaging more specifically, as it has been at the forefront of international trade and investment law disputes, while giving rise to other legal challenges. In what follows, we can see the interaction between different bodies of law and how they have been –or could be invoked – by relevant corporate actors to challenge regulation promoting the standardization of tobacco, alcohol, or food packaging to limit the appeal and therefore the consumption of commodities associated with ill health.

Two observations are important here. First, while each of these sets of legal challenges is formally distinct, as the legal obligations and systems relied upon are separate, there are important overlaps. For example, the protection of IP, including the use of trademarks on packaging, is protected in national legal orders – often as a result of commitments made under international trade law, not least the WTO Agreement on Trade-Related Aspects of Intellectual Property Rights (TRIPs Agreement). At the same time, the existence of IP receives protections under international investment agreements which protect the assets of investors, as IP is protected as a form of property. As such, these are linked and a single regulation can be challenged (or threatened to be challenged) in multiple systems at once, or one after another. This creates additional difficulties for governments, especially if they are resource constrained and find themselves responding to multiple challenges in multiple forums.

Second, while specific examples of formal legal challenge have been identified previously, most challenges take place before reaching a court or tribunal (whether national or international). This is common in legal practice, but mitigating such challenges often presents particular difficulties – that is, how best to identify lessons from the growing body of case law from different courts, tribunals and other dispute settlement bodies to best prepare for any explicit or implicit challenge to NCD prevention measures. It is increasingly clear that international trade and investment law are not, per se, obstacles to well-designed, evidence-based policy measures intended to prevent NCDs through the regulation of the tobacco, alcohol, and food industries.

The main lesson from the developing body of case law involving the relationship between international economic law, on the one hand, and public health protection, on the other hand, is not that governments can always act freely; rather, the successful cases of regulation have combined a willingness of governments to hold their position in the face of (formal or informal) challenges, with a commitment to defend such challenges, together with an awareness of the constraints that must be navigated to ensure that the legal challenges they face are effectively addressed and, ideally, averted altogether. This book has specifically been written in order to help governments maximize opportunities to effectively prevent NCDs by better understanding the constraints they face which are anchored in international trade and investment law.[23]

1.5 Other actors in the trade and health nexus

As the role of MNCs, especially in the tobacco, alcohol, and food industries, has been introduced previously, this section limits itself to briefly identifying the other relevant actors involved when analysing the relationship between international economic law and public health protection.

There is an assumed prioritization of businesses and their economic interests when discussing international economic law, as businesses are often the key beneficiaries of the system. It is traders rather than countries that trade, and in international economic relations, the role of the state is often to facilitate and support private actors, whether through improving conditions

---

[23] A Garde, 'Global Health Law and Non-Communicable Disease Prevention: Maximizing Opportunities by Understanding Constraints', in G Burci and B Toebes, *Research Handbook on Global Health Law* (Cheltenham: Edward Elgar, 2018) 420.

for economic activity or more concretely challenging specific barriers to trade. This makes international economic law fundamentally distinct from other areas of international law or policy, where the state is the focus. The institutions of the trade regime, not least governmental departments or international organizations such as the WTO, often play a supportive role to encourage trade. By contrast, the public health regime is understandably not centred around economic actors, but actors in the health and related sectors, including key international organizations, such as the WHO, and nongovernmental organizations (NGOs), including public health and consumer organizations.

1.6 The aims and structure of the chapters in this volume

In October 2017, states gathered in Montevideo to prepare the Third United Nations (UN) High-Level Meeting on NCDs where they repeated their 'commitment to take bold action and accelerate progress to, by 2030, reduce by one-third the premature mortality from [NCDs] in line with the 2030 Agenda for Sustainable Development'. For the first time, they explicitly acknowledged the need for legal expertise in this field, highlighting the relationship between NCDs and the law.[24]

This book contributes to legal capacity-building efforts by examining how governments can best operate within the constraints that international trade and investment law specifically may impose and effectively use their regulatory autonomy to promote better health for all. It is primarily intended for the public health community as an accessible introduction to the main international trade and investment law arguments that industry actors have used – or could use – to challenge the regulation of their products, commercial practices, and brands. It is also intended for an audience that

---

[24] UN General Assembly Resolution 73/2, September 2018, at para 21.4.

may be familiar with international economic law, but less so with the prevention of NCDs, as it reflects on how trade and investment law can best be approached to reconcile trade and health arguments, and therefore bridge the interdisciplinary divide we have so often observed in this field.

We do not attempt to provide a comprehensive legal account of the entirety of international economic law; more detailed texts exist elsewhere, and we have selected several of the best and most accessible in the Selected Bibliography. We have instead chosen to fundamentally reframe the host of legal obligations and their influence for public health actors by examining the principles that cut across the field. This novel approach marks a significant shift from traditional approaches to legal study, allowing us to explore critically important similarities and differences for policy actors in the content and practice of international economic law, not only in tribunals but also in the work of governments.

After presenting the sources and institutions of international trade law, and the law of the WTO more specifically (Chapter 2), we reflect in turn on the core principles of international trade law that directly relate to NCD prevention policies: the principle of transparency (Chapter 3), the principle of non-discrimination (Chapter 4), and the principle of necessity (Chapter 5). We then consider the principle of consistency through the development and role of international standards (Chapter 6) and then IP (Chapter 7), before turning to the other pillar of international economic law, namely international investment law (Chapter 8). We conclude with some thoughts on the future of health and trade policy, and how the public health community may be able to more effectively engage with international economic law to better prevent NCDs (Chapter 9).

1.6.1 Scope clarification

To provide an accurate but concise analysis, it was necessary to limit its scope. First, issues that could arise but have not arisen yet have been set to one side. In particular, trade in services is not discussed in detail here; we have chosen instead to focus primarily on the law on goods as more developed and more integrated than the law on services. That said, many of the principles underpinning the impact on international trade and investment law on trade in goods may also apply to services.

Second, we have also focused on certain types of NCD interventions, specifically those identified by the WHO 'best buys' and, within this group, taxation and packaging measures. This is because these measures have already given rise to extensive discussions within the context of international trade and investment law. Such measures also have clear trade implications, as they affect the costs incurred by traders wishing to operate in other jurisdictions than their own for packaging regulation, or lead to an increase in price for both packaging and taxation. Nonetheless, the book draws on a broader range of examples whenever this is useful for the argument.

Despite these limitations, by focusing on the operation of international economic law through a principle-based lens (predictability, non-discrimination, necessity, and consistency), the analysis presented is more easily transposable to other scenarios, in terms of both commercial practices and commodities (beyond tobacco, alcohol, and food to also include fossil fuels, pesticides, GMOs, gambling, vaping, and firearms). There will always be challenges when drawing from specific examples, stemming in particular from the complexity of the evidence base surrounding NCD prevention. As a result, it is necessary to carefully consider the specific circumstances and context surrounding a given measure to determine the outcome of a trade or investment dispute. At the same time, there are useful transferrable lessons that can be drawn from the experiences across NCD prevention and the much wider body of case law in international economic law and beyond, which this book aims to identify.

For the purposes of this book, we have defined the notion of 'food' broadly to include non-alcoholic beverages and breastmilk substitutes in order to refer to all food ingested throughout the life course. However, we need to clarify that health concerns primarily stem from the consumption of 'unhealthy food' – that is, nutritiously poor food that is high in fat, sugar, and salt and is often ultra-processed. We are aware of the debates surrounding the categorization of foods into 'healthy' or 'unhealthy' food, and the debates surrounding the contribution of ultra-processed foods to deteriorating food environments. These are not debates that we are proposing to revisit beyond recognizing the importance for governments to have robust, independent nutrient profiling systems in place to ensure that laws and regulations are underpinned by objective, evidence-based information.[25]

Ultimately, the challenge has been to provide a short introductory text that does not oversimplify the legal rules and principles of international trade and investment law. This is one area where the book's originality lies: in the careful selection of the material most relevant to the prevention of NCDs, framed and communicated through a principle-based approach. By placing the examination of the law in a practice-oriented policy context, we are able to provide a more accurate account of the role of international economic law for public health and a familiar context for policy actors. In this way, we hope this text will act as a reference point in the field, as we provide an accurate and accessible account of the complex worlds of NCD prevention and international economic law to readers, whether trade experts interested in health, health experts interested in trade, or any other academic or policy practitioners in the UK and beyond who may be interested in the relationship between these two complex but very significant worlds.

---

[25] This is not to suggest that nutrient profiling models do not provide fertile grounds for lengthy and costly legal challenges. For example, in the judicial review challenge it mounted against the 2021 Food (Promotion and Placement) (England) Regulations, Kellogg raised several questions concerning the UK Nutrient Profiling Model: *Kellogg v Secretary of State for Health and Social Care* [2022] EWHC 1710 (Admin).

TWO

The International Trade Law System and Public Health

2.1 Introduction

The most easily identifiable institution for international trade law is the World Trade Organization (WTO). As such, it constitutes the starting point for our analysis. This chapter introduces the international trade law system (section 2.2) and considers the law and institutions of the multilateral trade system at the WTO and how it accommodates the protection of public health (section 2.3), before introducing bilateral and regional trade agreements (free trade agreements, FTAs) (section 2.4). This allows us to start reflecting on the extent to which international trade law may constrain the regulatory autonomy of states to protect public health and prevent NCDs more specifically – the very question we consider from different, more specific perspectives in subsequent chapters.

2.2 An introduction to the World Trade Organization and its law

The WTO, headquartered in Geneva, is an international organization with 166 Members comprising both states and separate customs territories, including the EU, Hong Kong, Taiwan, and Macau.[1] The WTO was founded in 1995, after nearly a decade of negotiations to expand the scope and effectiveness of world trade rules beyond what had existed under the WTO's predecessor, the General Agreement on Tariffs and Trade (GATT) 1947, which had been introduced to liberalize trade in the post-Second World War period.

The WTO includes an institutional framework to develop binding rules, a place to share information, a forum to administer and monitor the compliance of governments with existing rules, and a place to resolve disputes. Importantly, its Secretariat has limited independent powers, and as such, what the WTO does – or does not do – depends on its Members. As such, it is often referred to as a 'Member-driven' organization.

Over 98 per cent of global trade is between WTO Members. The aim of the WTO is to liberalize trade in goods and services, in line with the needs and interests of its Members. Its objectives are clearly stated in the preamble to its constitutive treaty, the Agreement Establishing the World Trade Organization:[2]

> [Governments' action] in the field of trade and economic endeavour should be conducted with a view to raising standards of living, ensuring full employment and a large and steadily growing volume of real income and effective demand, and expanding the production of and trade in goods and services, while allowing for the optimal use of the world's resources in accordance with the objective of sustainable development, seeking both to protect and preserve the environment and to enhance the means for doing so in a manner consistent with their respective needs and concerns at different levels of economic

---

[1] This is a peculiar feature of the WTO: Article XII.1 of the Agreement Establishing the World Trade Organization (sometimes referred to as the 'Marrakesh Agreement' or simply the 'WTO Agreement').

[2] Preamble to the WTO Agreement.

development ... by entering into reciprocal and mutually advantageous arrangements directed to the substantial reduction of tariffs and other barriers to trade and to the eliminations of discriminatory treatment in international trade relations.[3]

Notably, this provision highlights the importance of non-discrimination and of reducing barriers to trade, but also sustainable development, the interests of developing country Members, and raising standards of living and ensuring full employment, all of which – in different ways – speak to the concerns and interests of the public health community.

Beyond the preamble to the WTO Agreement, the rules of the institution refer to public health in multiple ways:

- One of the key provisions of WTO law – Article XX(b) GATT – relates to the right of governments to introduce measures 'necessary to protect human, animal or plant life or health'.
- WTO case law has often recognized the right of governments to promote legitimate public interests such as human health.[4]
- The membership of the WTO has explicitly confirmed the right of Members to protect public health, whether in IP rights in the 2001 Declaration on the TRIPs Agreement and Public Health (the Doha Declaration), or the more recent 2022 Ministerial Declaration on the WTO Response to the COVID-19 Pandemic and Preparedness for Future Pandemics.

As we consider how governments can prevent NCDs and protect public health, it is helpful to clarify the nature of the limits that international trade law places upon them,

---

[3] Preamble to the WTO Agreement.
[4] For example, Panel Report, *Brazil – Retreaded Tyres* (DS332), para 7.108.

considering the recurring discussions on 'regulatory autonomy', the protection of 'policy space', and the 'right to regulate' for governments, so they can pursue legitimate public interest objectives, including the protection of public health.

A key point of clarification is needed here. It is not that international trade law carves out a space for governments to pursue public policies which are important to them. As a matter of international law, states are *entitled* to act as they wish and are *only* limited by commitments they have entered into consensually or by virtue of being part of the international legal order.[5] This has been unequivocally confirmed by the Appellate Body in a seminal dispute where the US was challenged on restrictions it introduced on trade in shrimp in order to protect the environment, and endangered sea turtles more specifically. The US lost, in part, due to the inconsistent way in which its environmental measures were introduced. Although the Appellate Body was at pains to note the legitimacy of the objectives of the US, it noted:

> In reaching these conclusions, we wish to underscore what we have not decided in this appeal. We have not decided that the protection and preservation of the environment is of no significance to the Members of the WTO. Clearly, it is. We have not decided that the sovereign nations that are Members of the WTO cannot adopt effective measures to protect endangered species, such as sea turtles. Clearly, they can and should. And

---

5   *The Case of the SS Lotus* (1927), PCIJ Series A – No 10, p 18: 'International law governs relations between independent States. The rules of law binding upon States therefore emanate from their own free will as expressed in conventions or by usages generally accepted as expressing principles of law and established in order to regulate the relations between these co-existing independent communities or with a view to the achievement of common aims. Restrictions upon the independence of States cannot therefore be presumed.'

we have not decided that sovereign states should not act together bilaterally, plurilaterally or multilaterally, either within the WTO or in other international forums, to protect endangered species or to otherwise protect the environment. Clearly, they should and do.

WTO Members are free to adopt their own policies aimed at protecting the environment as long as, in so doing, they fulfil their obligations and respect the rights of other Members under WTO law.[6]

As we shall see in the following chapters, WTO law sets out requirements for how Members must apply their policy measures, including NCD prevention measures, but this does not stop them from preventing NCDs: this is indeed a legitimate policy objective. In most cases – and very importantly for our purposes – the commitments are interpreted in light of the importance of these policy objectives.[7] We have ample examples where the importance of protecting public health has been noted as 'both vital and important in the highest degree'.[8]

Therefore, it is not that governments can tackle NCDs only within the policy space left to them by their international commitments, but rather that they are entitled to do so as long as they do not violate their obligations. Additionally, the introduction of measures to prevent NCDs is, in most cases, not an additional 'extra' for a government, but rather a legal requirement under international human rights law.

The existence of a human rights obligation on a WTO Member to make efforts to prevent NCDs, not least to protect children and other particularly vulnerable groups, does not give that government carte blanche to act as they wish. International

---

[6] Report of the Appellate Body, *US – Shrimp* (DS58), paras 185–186.

[7] Whether incorporated in legal analysis as 'necessity' under Article XX(b) GATT, or the 'legitimate objective' of the measures under the TBT Agreement, and so on.

[8] Panel Report, *Brazil – Retreaded Tyres* (DS332), para 7.210.

obligations are cumulative, and governments will need to comply with all relevant obligations (that is, both human rights and trade law). While the position of international trade law vis-à-vis human rights law is a contested and much discussed topic, these two bodies of law form part of the same international legal order. And in the context of WTO dispute settlement, the Appellate Body has been clear, from its very first report, that trade law 'is not to be read in clinical isolation from public international law'.[9]

Reliance on human right-based arguments will not work by themselves in international trade law, but the ability of governments to easily identify the *legitimacy* and *importance* of their aim is legally helpful, and – importantly – a strategically powerful tool for framing their claims in both formal legal proceedings and other forums where governments engage with each other, including committees and informal dialogues, as will be discussed later on.

Therefore, the relationship between trade and public health does not have to be confrontational, as is sometimes claimed, with governments choosing either to protect health or to support trade. Instead, the relationship can be envisaged as mutually supportive, reflecting the importance of public health in and for trade. This crucial point is a recurring theme of our analysis.[10]

2.3 The institutions of the WTO and its rules

The WTO is home to a range of bodies, committees, working groups, and a dispute settlement mechanism, all designed to support the work of its Members. As we have already noted,

---

[9] Report of the Appellate Body, *US – Gasoline* (DS2), p 17.

[10] The concept of 'mutual supportiveness' has been most developed in the relationship between trade policy and the environment, dating back to 1992: Agenda 21, at para 2.3(b): www.un.org/esa/dsd/agenda21/res_agenda21_00.shtml

Figure 2.1: The WTO institutional structure

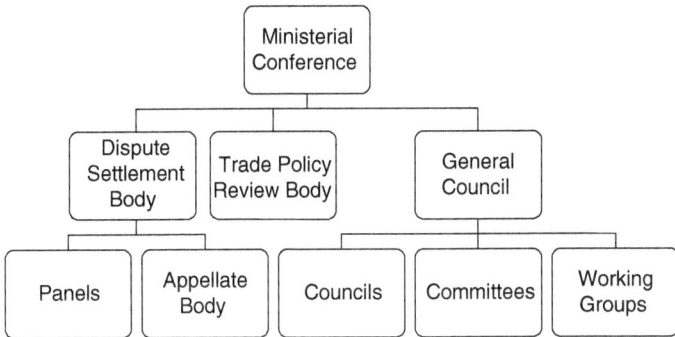

the WTO is often described as a 'Member-driven' organization. This is most noticeable in its institutional framework as all Members can sit in all groups and committees, and are the drivers of the WTO's governance through its bodies. Figure 2.1 provides a map of the key institutions of the WTO.

The Ministerial Conference, which meets roughly every two years, sits at the 'top' of the system to adopt new rules (or not) and give overarching political direction.

The day-to-day governance of the WTO is managed by a set of subsidiary bodies that sit below the Ministerial Conference. A tripartite division helps to ensure that the principal functions of the WTO are fulfilled:

- the General Council focuses on negotiations, monitoring, and political direction (section 2.3.1);
- the Trade Policy Review Body promotes transparency (section 2.3.2); and
- the Dispute Settlement Body settles legal disputes between WTO Members (section 2.3.3).

In practice, the General Council and the Trade Policy Review Body are composed of the same attendees, usually ambassadors/heads of mission or their deputies. The Dispute

Settlement Body is mostly attended by senior lawyers from Members' delegations.

2.3.1 A home for the rules of international trade

One, if not *the* most important, function of the WTO is to host a comprehensive set of rules that govern the behaviour of governments concerning international trade. These 'covered agreements'[11] include the original GATT 1947 with some adjustments (incorporated formally as the GATT 1994), as well as rules on the regulation of goods (for example, technical barriers to trade [TBT]), on intellectual property (TRIPS), subsidies, unexpected import surges, predatory pricing, services, customs valuation, rules of origin, and many more. This is why WTO law is so important from the perspective of tackling NCDs: its obligations for governments touch on multiple different preventive measures, including labelling, packaging, marketing, and pricing measures. As WTO commitments apply to the whole of government activity, they are not only the concern of trade departments or ministries. Intra-government coherence of action is therefore crucial to ensure that trade, health, and other policies are aligned. Moreover, for those WTO Members that have constituent parts, states, or regions (such as the devolved nations in the UK or the Member States of the EU), these rules also apply to them. WTO commitments are therefore both wide (applying to many issues across policy areas) and deep (applying throughout the territory of WTO Members).[12]

---

[11] So called because they are covered by the dispute settlement mechanism of the WTO and thus legally enforceable.

[12] The is explicitly noted in Article XVI of the WTO Agreement, which reflects, in part, the rule under general international law (codified in Article 27 of the Vienna Convention on the Law of Treaties 1969) that: 'A party may not invoke the provisions of its internal law as justification for its failure to perform a treaty.'

The early focus in international trade law on improving trade, particularly in the postwar period, was to control the use by countries of tariffs, that is, border taxes such as customs duties or other charges imposed on goods traded across borders.[13] Additionally, and importantly for our purposes, international trade law introduced a series of general rules and principles, including obligations prohibiting discrimination in trade policy and those ensuring that national rules do not restrict trade more than is necessary to achieve the legitimate objectives they pursue, not least the protection of public health. These obligations remain central to many international trade rules, as will be discussed in the following chapters.

By the 1980s, the focus on trade liberalization had shifted away from tariffs, which had been significantly reduced since the creation of the GATT in 1947. Many rules today focus on what governments do within their territory when regulating or taxing. They include commitments relating not only to goods, but also to services and IP.

As outlined in Table 2.1, the WTO covered agreements cut across a swathe of government activity, and therefore have significant relevance for the regulation of NCDs.

---

[13] In this sentence we refer to countries ('states' in formal international law terminology). However, throughout the book, we will mainly refer to governments as key actors of international economic law. This is not formally correct as a matter of law: the state and the government are not necessarily the same (for example, there may be recognized governments in exile, such as the Latvian government during the Soviet occupation). However, as we have noted previously, it is not only 'countries' that are members of international economic law agreements: the EU (an international organization) is a founding Member of the WTO, but is not a 'state' for the purposes of international law. Nor are Hong Kong, Taiwan, and Macau, which are also WTO Members. We have settled on 'governments' to identify actors that govern trade relations, though we are aware of the limitations such choices unavoidably entail.

Table 2.1: The relevance of WTO agreements for NCDs

Covered agreement	Purpose	Relevance for NCDs
General Agreement on Tariffs & Trade (GATT)	To encourage international trade in goods by restricting the use of discriminatory measures, improving certainty in conditions of trade, and protecting the regulatory autonomy of governments	Many, including prevention policies which rely on internal taxes (such as excise duties or industry levies imposed on tobacco, alcohol, and unhealthy food), or which restrict the importation or sale of goods
Agreement on Technical Barriers to Trade (TBT)	Reduce regulatory barriers to trade, encourage harmonization of regulatory approaches, and safeguard governments' pursuit of legitimate regulatory objectives	Many NCD prevention policies will fall within the scope of the TBT Agreement. They include NCD prevention policies regulating product packaging such as: health warning labels on tobacco, alcohol, or unhealthy food; mandated back or front-of-pack nutrition labelling (FoPNL); claims regulation (prohibition of claims on tobacco or alcoholic beverages, and regulation of nutrition and health claims on food); prohibition of the use of packaging as a marketing tool (for example, imposition of tobacco plain packaging, prohibition of the use of cartoon or equity brand characters popular with children, or the use of celebrities, prohibition of certain packaging shapes, and prohibition of the offer of free toys within the packaging)

Table 2.1: The relevance of WTO agreements for NCDs (continued)

Covered agreement	Purpose	Relevance for NCDs
Agreement on Sanitary & Phytosanitary Measures (SPS)	As with the TBT Agreement, but with a particular focus on policies intended to combat pests, disease-causing organisms, toxins, and contaminants	Prevention policies which restrict the importation or sale of products with toxins and other food safety measures (for example, regulation of the use of food additives, food flavourings that are commonly food in ultra-processed foods)
Agreement on Trade-Related Aspects of Intellectual Property Rights (TRIPS)	Improve the protection of IP rights globally	Prevention policies which could interfere with the use of trademarks (for example, plain packaging, claims regulation and other marketing restrictions, mandatory disclosure requirements, such as textual or pictorial health warnings, FoPNL, ingredient declaration, limitations on the use of equity brand characters and so on)
General Agreement on Trade in Services (GATS)	Improve international trade in services by restricting the use of discriminatory measures, improving certainty in conditions of trade, and protecting the regulatory autonomy of governments	Prevention policies that restrict relevant services such as marketing or advertising, including on digital platforms

The WTO has been less successful in negotiating *new* rules since its creation. Agreement at the WTO is made by consensus (that is, the absence of an objection by a Member in attendance),[14] and a limited number of Members have blocked agreement over the years by refusing to 'join the consensus', leading to deadlock at the WTO. If there have been some successes, most notably the conclusion of an Agreement on Fisheries Subsidies in June 2022, there are still gaps within the trade regime relating both to long-running concerns, including access to medicines, and to more recent areas of interest, such as trade in plastics.

In the face of deadlock, groups of WTO Members have negotiated new commitments among themselves. These 'plurilaterals' have included agreements on additional liberalization of information technology (IT) products, commitments on domestic regulation of services, e-commerce, and ongoing structured discussions on trade and sustainable development.[15] Importantly, WTO Members have also pursued preferential trade agreements through FTAs, as will be discussed later on.

Beyond the new rules introduced, the WTO has established an institutional framework which has had a lasting impact on the international trade system. In particular, the WTO committee structure provides an ongoing forum for governments to monitor each other's policies and to engage over potential trade disputes, including when they represent industry's concerns on their behalf, as well as an effective system for early dispute settlement – with teeth, and for all its failings, more effective than most other international law dispute settlement systems. The imperative to avoid challenges

---

14 Formally, voting is available, but the practice of the organization is to take decisions by consensus. Explicit reference to this is made in Article IX:1 of the WTO Agreement.

15 These agreements cannot create obligations for nonparties. Their increasing use is subject to debate in some quarters (for example, India's view that the negotiation and conclusion of Investment Facilitation for Development plurilateral agreement was illegal: WT/GC/262).

to national policies necessarily pushes government inclination to take international trade law very seriously.

2.3.2 A place to discuss and monitor trade policies

As we have noted, one of the key functions of the WTO is to act as a forum for Members to discuss relevant trade issues. This is enabled through transparency mechanisms that are designed to improve access to information on the activities of governments. Some processes of information sharing and peer review are elaborate. The Trade Policy Review Mechanism periodically allows WTO Members to question other Members on any aspect of their international trade policy, offering them a chance to raise issues concerning specific measures as well as more general issues relating to the reviewed Member's trade policy.[16] More broadly, the process of improving transparency and access to information is consistent throughout the WTO and happens on a more frequent basis, most notably through notifications and committees.

The WTO is home to an elaborate network of over 40 committees, councils, and working groups. Each one covers the work of a specialised agreement (for example, the Council for Trade-Related Aspects of Intellectual Property Rights [TRIPS Council]) or a set of issues (for example, the Committee on Trade and the Environment). For our purposes, the Committee on Technical Barriers to Trade (the TBT Committee) is of particular interest for at least two reasons: first, its remit covers critically important NCD prevention measures, including all those

---

[16] The frequency of reviews is determined by the size of the Member's economy, with the US, EU, Japan, and China being reviewed every three years, the next 16 largest Members every five years, and the remaining Members every seven years. Trade Policy Reviews provide an excellent source of information for those interested in finding out more about a specific WTO Member's trade policy. See https://www.wto.org/engl ish/tratop_e/tpr_e/tpr_e.htm

regulating tobacco, alcohol, or food labelling and packaging; and, second, it is one of the more developed committees in creating a system whereby Members notify regulatory measures which can then be discussed by interested or concerned Members.

The TBT Committee

The TBT Agreement has its own committee, the role of which is to provide a forum where governments introducing new technical regulations, including those with the objective of protecting public health and preventing NCDs, can be discussed. Governments are usually represented by officials they send from their capitals, those based in Geneva, or both. The TBT Committee typically meets three or four times a year.

All WTO Members must notify the TBT Committee of any new technical barrier to trade which may have a significant impact on international trade. Consequently, the Committee becomes a clearing house for potential conflicting interests between Members that want to introduce certain types of new public health measures, those that are opposed to them, and those that are not opposed to the measures per se, but have concerns over the measure's design. Between 1 January 1995 and 1 April 2024, 53,610 notifications were made to the TBT Committee.

A key feature of the TBT Committee is the ability of Members to raise 'specific trade concerns' (STCs), namely specific questions of over the potential compliance of a Member's notified measure with WTO law. These concerns must be addressed in the TBT Committee, and form an important step in signalling that a Member may need to consider revising or withdrawing its proposed regulation. Between 1 January 1995 and 1 April 2024, 828 STCs were raised at the TBT Committee.

Unresolved issues in the TBT Committee (or another committee) may escalate to formal dispute, as will be discussed later on. However, this only happens in a handful of cases: 57 TBT disputes were initiated between 1 January 1995 and 1 April 2024, of which 11 led to a ruling.

Most governments are not able to monitor all new regulatory measures on the horizon across the globe or know how or why new measures may or may not affect the commercial interests of traders in their territory. As such, traders routinely communicate with governments.[17] In most instances this dynamic is to be expected – the WTO system is designed to encourage trade. However, as noted in Chapter 1, where there is an overriding public policy interest that is not in the commercial interest of traders to raise, this presents serious challenges for governments that must be mitigated. This is particularly important for public health measures challenged at the WTO, as the WTO has become a key site of contestation.

2.3.3 Dispute settlement

As we have seen, the WTO is home to a body of rules and a place where Members discuss their application. It is also home to a system designed to *enforce* those rules. While litigation is rare, the existence of an effective system which can be relied upon to enforce rights and obligations is extremely important to ensure compliance with WTO law. This is particularly so, as the WTO dispute settlement system is historically comparatively effective. Unlike most international organizations, it requires that all Members consent to jurisdiction as a condition of their membership, *always* allowing any Member to raise a formal dispute and having a panel of experts hear their claims against another.[18] Additionally, parties can appeal the reports of these panels to a standing tribunal: the Appellate Body.[19] This may

---

[17] Whether through lobbyists, representative organizations, or directly in their capital or through embassies.

[18] Most commonly, panellists are expert trade lawyers, though there are exceptions. For example, one of the panellists on the *Costa Rica – Avocados (Mexico)* (DS524) dispute over an infectious disease effecting avocados was an agricultural health and food safety specialist.

[19] The Appellate Body is not currently able to hear appeals as it has insufficient members appointed to it. This is the result of US complaints

seem trivial, since we presume, in a national context, that courts can hear disputes between private parties over, for example, a contractual dispute. However, in international law, which is based on the consent of states, this type of quasi-compulsory jurisdiction is rare.[20] Finally, reports of panels or the Appellate Body are adopted by the Dispute Settlement Body, representing all WTO Members. Adoption of reports is de facto automatic. These adopted reports become an important element of WTO law as they set out (often at great length) how the law has been interpreted in instances where it is unclear or debated.

Where two WTO Members disagree, and this cannot be resolved through negotiation, the process is as follows (see Figure 2.2).

On paper, this is faster and more efficient than dispute settlement in most other areas of international law. Access to the Appellate Body is important as it is a standing body and ensures that the interpretation given to the covered agreements by panels is (relatively) consistent. In cases where a Member does not comply with the findings of a panel or Appellate Body report, the injured party can be authorised to 'retaliate'. Between 1 January 1995 and 28 June 2024, there were 624 requests for consultations (the first step in a formal dispute) and over 292 panel reports were circulated.[21]

Despite its active use by WTO Members, we note that this process (outlined in Figure 2.3) faces several challenges.

First, retaliation (usually in the form of tariffs) is not always effective – if you are not a significant importer of any products or are largely dependent on the noncompliant partner for all your trade, you are in a weak position. Financial compensation

---

over the WTO dispute settlement system and has had a disruptive effect on the ability of WTO Members to use the system with confidence.

[20] However, it should be noted that it is also found in many international investment agreements, as discussed in Chapter 8.

[21] By point of comparison, the International Court of Justice has delivered fewer than 180 since its creation in 1946.

Figure 2.2: The formal WTO dispute settlement process

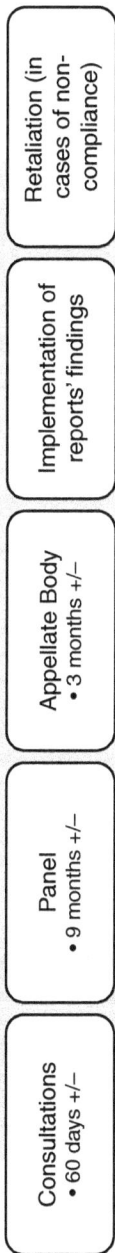

Figure 2.3: The WTO dispute settlement process in practice

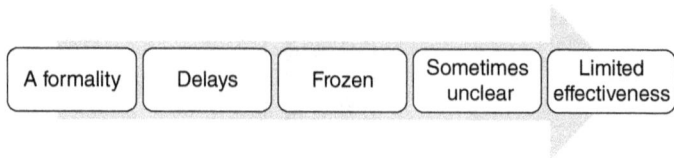

A formality	Delays	Frozen	Sometimes unclear	Limited effectiveness

does not exist at the WTO, so the type of countermeasure (and, indeed, the settlement that parties reach) sits squarely in the world of intergovernmental negotiations and trade-offs.

Second, while panel reports should be delivered within nine months, they are often delayed due to the complexity of disputes. For example, in the *Australia – Tobacco Plain Packaging* dispute, the Panel was established on 26 March 2014, but its report was circulated over four years later on 28 June 2018. The Appellate Body report was released two years later on 9 June 2020.

Third, and most importantly, the Appellate Body is currently nonfunctional due to a lack of Members – in effect, judges – as the US has been blocking new appointments. This has created a serious problem for the system: where a WTO Member loses at the panel stage, they can appeal, but in the absence of the Appellate Body to hear the dispute, the report is never adopted and parties 'appeal into the void'.[22] As a consequence, the report is not formally binding and no countermeasures can be authorized.[23]

---

[22] Technically, reports from panels and the Appellate Body are not legally binding until they are adopted by the Dispute Settlement Body. This is a de facto automatic process as the only way for a report not to be adopted is if all Members (including the winning party) reject it. However, in the case of appeals, the panel report is not sent to the Dispute Settlement Body until the Appellate Body report is published. Of course, this means that where there is no Appellate Body to hear a dispute, the panel report is never adopted.

[23] Some WTO Members have sought ways to fix this until such a time as the Appellate Body can be restored, but there are key players where this is still not the case (not least the US).

Despite all its shortcomings, the dispute settlement system of the WTO is still used. The international community is fundamentally a shame-based social order, and Members are loath to appear non-compliant with international trade law, unless there is a strong overriding interest at play. Litigation is rare, as much (more informal) dispute settlement sits in the day-to-day engagement between WTO Members at, and in the margins of, committees and through their representatives bilaterally. Nevertheless, the spectre of its use is an important factor to consider in the contestation of public health measures through international trade law institutions.

2.4 Other institutions of the international trade regime: free trade agreements

Although the WTO acts as the central nexus for information and intergovernmental interactions in trade, it is not the only institution strategically used by governments. All WTO Members (to varying degrees) have concluded FTAs.

As noted previously, it has become increasingly difficult to negotiate new rules at the WTO that apply to the whole membership. Governments have therefore pursued agreements between themselves. FTAs are, in many ways, antithetical to the WTO: whereas the WTO prioritizes multilateral, non-discriminatory trade liberalization, FTAs – by their very nature – are discriminatory, as they allow two or more WTO Members to give each other improved market access and benefits that they do not give to others. In order to balance the desire to encourage multilateral trade liberalization, on the one hand, and the recognition that some Members will want to move more quickly between themselves, on the other hand, the GATT places requirements on the creation of FTAs. Specifically, any FTA must liberalize 'substantially all the trade' between the parties.[24] While

---

[24] Article XXIV:8 GATT.

parties to FTAs grant each other preferences they do not grant others, the WTO remains an important baseline and institution for their trading relations.

FTAs are legally distinct agreements from the WTO: although they are related, they do not share institutions (for example, committees) and must therefore set up their own. The UK's FTAs, for example, have required the creation over 80 such committees with its various FTA partners to discuss issues under their agreement, from trade in goods, to IP and subsidies.

Most FTAs are bilateral (for example, the EU–Japan Economic Partnership Agreement), although trilateral (for example, the US, Mexico, Canada Trade Agreement [USMCA]) and regional FTAs also exist (for example, the Comprehensive and Progressive TransPacific Partnership [CPTPP] or the African Continental Free Trade Agreement [ACFTA]). Though FTAs vary in scope and depth of liberalization, they share certain commonalities.

Typically, FTAs will include multiple sections (or 'chapters') dealing with substantive issues of trade liberalization (tariffs, regulation, taxation and so on) while others will focus on institutional elements (such as establishing committees or dispute settlement mechanisms).

Some of these chapters include commitments that exist at the WTO, but go further – for example, lower tariffs to zero tariffs, improving market access to healthcare, or increasing protections for pharmaceutical patents. These commitments are sometimes called 'WTO+', as they cover the same substance as the WTO, but go further.[25] Other commitments, such as those on labour rights, environmental protection, and sustainable development, are often called 'WTO-X' commitments, as they are something not currently covered (in this way) at the

---

[25]   C Hofmann, A Osnago, and M Ruta, 'The Content of Preferential Trade Agreements', *World Trade Review* 18(3) (2019) 365.

WTO.[26] In the case of 'WTO+' commitments, there will be an overlap with WTO rules and therefore where an issue arises at the WTO, it is likely to also arise under the relevant FTA(s). Thus, although formally separate, in truth governments monitor their commitments under the WTO and all their FTAs simultaneously.

Australia's relationship with the UK is an interesting case in point: both are WTO Members, parties to CPTPP, and have a bilateral FTA. Each of these agreements has its own institutional framework with committees and dispute settlement mechanisms, and each has its own commitments (which vary across the three), but for these two countries, their commitments are cumulative and, in some places, overlap. For example, if the UK decided to impose restrictions on the importation of unhealthy food which would affect Australia, it would need to be able to justify these measures under WTO law, under CPTPP, and under the Australia-UK FTA, relying on the specific rules in each of those.

Therefore, it is important not to see these different institutions or agreements as existing in isolation from each other, but instead as part of a single larger picture. This is also true in the forums where issues are raised or measures challenged. We have noted that WTO Members raise concerns under WTO committees; they do so too under the comparable structures of FTAs. FTAs therefore offer governments (and thus, indirectly, also private actors) another set of institutions with which to engage, often with different underlying power dynamics.

For example, the UK has challenged Peru's internal taxation regime on the ground that it gives domestically produced *pisco* a competitive advantage over imported gin and whisky. This has been raised through bilateral discussions from the UK's embassy in Lima, through committees under

---

[26] C Hofmann, A Osnago and M Ruta, 'The Content of Preferential Trade Agreements', *World Trade Review* 18(3) (2019) 365.

the UK-Andean FTA and, more recently, at the WTO Committee on Market Access and subsequently the Council on Trade in Goods, in what is expected to be the final step ahead of a formal legal dispute.[27] Monitoring what happens across all these bodies is a challenge, but it is nonetheless important to ensure that public health and other legitimate interests are not lost from sight.

2.5 Conclusions

In formal terms, international trade law is primarily intergovernmental. However, in practice, governments are far from the only relevant players. Whether international organizations such as the WHO or the WTO, or businesses whose interests may be disadvantaged by new regulation, or civil society groups that are trying to represent the voices of citizens, we cannot only look at governments to understand the dynamics at play in international trade law forums; we also need to bear in mind the actors identified earlier in Chapter 1.

This chapter has introduced the overarching framework that regulates trade with public health policy actors in mind. These institutions are a key part of how the system can be used, at best, to support public health objectives or, at least, to ensure that they do not undermine the legitimate objectives of the public health community. In the following chapters, we examine what international economic law requires of governments. Some of the principles on which it is based do present genuine limitations on what governments can and cannot do. However, as will be demonstrated throughout this book, it is important to understand from the outset that robust public health policies *can* be pursued in compliance with both

---

[27] See: '21 to 22 July 2022: Joint Minutes of the first UK-Andean Trade Committee', updated 6 September 2024; WTO Committee on Market Access, 'Formal Meeting of 16–17 October 2023' (G/MA/M/79).

international trade law and international investment law. At the heart of this short book is the argument that governments can maximise opportunities to effectively prevent NCDs and therefore promote better health for all by better understanding the (limited) constraints that international economic law imposes on them.

THREE

The Principle of Predictability

3.1 Introduction

International economic affairs depend on a degree of predictability. For businesses, the transparency and stability of trading conditions, regulatory frameworks, and treatment by governments are an important part of their strategic planning. This is why the WTO's own dispute settlement system is explicitly intended to be 'a central element in providing security and predictability to the multilateral trading system'.[1]

International trade rules reflect the fact that circumstances change, and governments may wish to address new issues. Stability understood as the maintenance of a status quo is neither possible nor desirable. That said, changes in trading conditions are largely expected to take place considering the interests of affected parties, including those of other WTO Members.[2] This is why international trade law requires that WTO Members notify others when they regulate, including

---

[1] Article 3.2 of the Dispute Settlement Understanding (DSU).
[2] For example, Article 7 and Annex B of the WTO Agreement on Sanitary and Phytosanitary Measures.

in response to public health challenges, which may have an impact on trade. Importantly, such notification requirements do not prevent governments from acting; rather, they aim to promote transparency. Consequently, governments need to be well prepared before adopting new laws and policies, both in terms of the evidence base underpinning these laws and policies, and their strategy for engaging with public and private actors.

Figure 3.1 shows where predictability is relevant for the range of NCD prevention measures identified in Chapter 1. In this chapter, we explore how predictability plays a role across multiple policy instruments, including in relation to tariffs (section 3.2), notification and consultation requirements (section 3.3), and regulatory cooperation under FTAs (section 3.4).

3.2 Tariffs

One of the clearest examples of predictability relates to tariffs. Article II GATT requires WTO Members to maintain lists of products where they commit not to exceed a certain tariff for each specific good under their 'schedules'. Schedules are annexed to the GATT, although they are, by virtue of Article II GATT, an integral part of the GATT and are legally binding. These documents include extensive lists of products, divided by tariff classification, a numerical value assigned to each product. Among others, schedules set out the WTO Member's 'bound' tariff – that is, the cap over which, absent an exception, they cannot raise their tariffs.

Many Members have no interest in having such high tariffs, as they see the benefit of lower tariffs in reducing prices for consumers and enhancing competition. Therefore, WTO law allows them to lower their tariffs to what is known as the 'applied' rate. If tariffs are at the 'applied' rate, they must be applied equally to all other WTO Members: each WTO Member is entitled to the same treatment as the most-favoured

Figure 3.1: Points in the supply chain where information is sought by economic actors

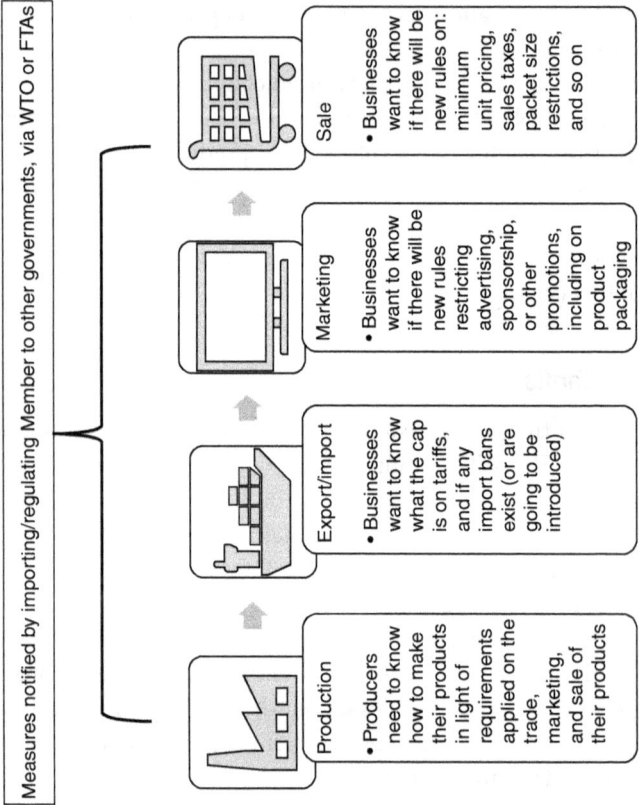

Measures notified by importing/regulating Member to other governments, via WTO or FTAs

Production
- Producers need to know how to make their products in light of requirements applied on the trade, marketing, and sale of their products

Export/import
- Businesses want to know what the cap is on tariffs, and if any import bans exist (or are going to be introduced)

Marketing
- Businesses want to know if there will be new rules restricting advertising, sponsorship, or other promotions, including on product packaging

Sale
- Businesses want to know if there will be new rules on: minimum unit pricing, sales taxes, packet size restrictions, and so on

nation (MFN).[3] We will discuss MFN and its main exceptions in Chapter 4.

In any event, whether the government applies the highest tariff (the bound rate) or a lower tariff (the applied rate), it must apply this tariff to imports of this product from all other WTO Members. This can present serious challenges for alcohol or unhealthy – often cheaper – food, as Samoa's ban on turkey tails illustrates.[4]

The tale of Samoa's ban on turkey tails and its accession to the WTO

As part of the process that led to its accession to the WTO in May 2012, Samoa had to agree its tariff schedule. Article XII of the WTO Agreement sets out the initial requirements for accession, stating that the Ministerial Conference takes decisions on accession of new Members, subject to a two-third majority. However, in practice, consensus is the overriding practice of the institution. Therefore, in order to join the WTO, in effect, all Members must agree. This gives considerable negotiating capital to those that have sufficient economic and political power to block the entry of a new Member.

Samoa intended to maintain a ban on 'turkey tails' – a cheap fatty meat often exported to developing countries, but it faced significant pushback. While import and export bans are generally prohibited under WTO law, there are limited public policy exceptions, including the protection of human health.[5] Therefore, in this instance, Samoa stressed the public health nature of its concerns, as one of the countries with some of the highest rates of NCDs in the world. It received the support of the WHO and others. However, given the stringent requirements of meeting the conditions under the

---

[3] Article I GATT.
[4] AM Thow et al, 'Food Supply, Nutrition and Trade Policy: Reversal of an Import Ban on Turkey Tails', *Bulletin of the World Health Organization* 95(10) (2017) 723.
[5] Article XI(1), XI(2) and XX GATT respectively.

exception provisions of the GATT, and the overwhelming opposition to Samoa's existing ban by several WTO Members, it was agreed that Samoa would progressively remove the ban, replacing it with a tariff of 300 per cent, reduced to 100 per cent and subsequently reduced further.

One can argue that Samoa only needed to bind its tariffs at a very high level, as it did for a period, to discourage imports of turkey tails. The rules of the WTO do not require a progressive lowering of tariffs – though negotiations to this effect are encouraged and recognized as being 'of great importance.'[6] However, this ignores the practice of international trade relations, where exporting Members exert *ongoing* pressure to reduce tariffs. As a result, rather than maintaining a clear import ban, Samoa transitioned to a high tariff on turkey tails and has then been subjected to *continued* pressure to reduce tariffs.

3.2.1 Tariffs and free trade agreements

FTAs have a similar dynamic also requiring tariff commitments. This is particularly so as FTAs are required to liberalize 'substantially all the trade' between the parties, which has been interpreted to mean tariff reductions of near-to-zero on most products.[7] For businesses, the commitments under FTAs provide an important additional element of security and predictability, supporting the planning of their operations by reducing the risk that a trading partner increases a low applied tariff to its WTO 'bound' tariff.

---

6 Article XXVIII bis GATT.

7 As FTAs provide preferences to some trading partners over others, they would normally constitute a violation of non-discrimination commitments (particularly Article I GATT, 'most-favoured nation', which we will discuss further in Chapter 4). Thus, Article XXIV GATT acts as an exception, subject to the parties liberalizing greatly – as a form of quid pro quo for what would otherwise be a discriminatory measure.

3.3 Beyond tariffs: notifications and consultation requirements for regulatory measures

Once goods have entered a market, and any tariffs have been incurred, these goods must still comply with the law in force in that market. For example, a cigarette manufacturer cannot sell cigarettes in the UK if they do not meet the requirements of UK law, including those mandating tobacco plain packaging and combined (pictorial and textual) health warnings. Ensuring that such regulatory, or 'behind-the-border', measures are known to Members, and therefore the businesses operating within their borders, constitutes an important part of WTO law. The GATT and the TBT Agreement are both critical when regulating the tobacco, alcohol, and food industries to prevent NCDs. So is the TRIPS Agreement, which we will discuss specifically in Chapter 7.

Exporting businesses want to know (1) what rules apply in each market, and (2) whether those rules are about to change, so that they can adjust their production or distribution processes, where necessary, to meet the new requirements in export markets. This is why notification and consultation obligations are particularly important to promote predictability. Under many WTO agreements, not least the TBT Agreement, WTO Members are required to notify other Members of their proposed measures.[8]

It should be noted that not everything governments do needs to be notified to the WTO or to FTA partners. Importantly, a measure needs to potentially affect international trade to fall within the purview of WTO law and be subject, as such, to a notification obligation. In each case, the specific commitments under the relevant agreement will determine what to notify. For example, mandatory rules on how products are to be

---

[8] There are instances where measures are notified *after* they are introduced, but this is rare; this is only permitted for emergency measures (for example, certain measures were notified on this basis during the COVID-19 pandemic).

Table 3.1: Notification requirements under the TBT Agreement

TBT Agreement	Requirement
Article 2.9	Where a new technical regulation is 'not based on an existing international standard'
Article 2.9	And it 'may have a significant effect on trade of other Members'
Article 2.9.1	Publish that 'they propose to introduce a particular technical regulation'
Article 2.9.3	'Upon request' provide 'particulars or copies' of the proposed technical regulation
Article 2.9.5	'[A]llow reasonable time for other Members to make comments in writing, discuss these comments upon request, and take these written comments and the results of these discussions into account'

packaged (for example, mandating tobacco plain packaging, alcohol health warnings, or FoPNL) are 'technical regulations' for the purposes of the TBT Agreement and may require notification as shown in Table 3.1.[9]

The TBT Committee has provided additional guidance on some of these elements, including what may have a 'significant effect on trade'.[10] Panels have further interpreted the scope of WTO Members' notification obligations, confirming that the effect on trade of the proposed measure 'does not require proving actual trade effects. Rather, this condition encompasses

---

[9] Annex 1(1) of the TBT Agreement: 'Document which lays down product characteristics or their related processes and production methods, including the applicable administrative provisions, *with which compliance is mandatory*. It may also include or deal exclusively with terminology, symbols, packaging, marking or labelling requirements as they apply to a product, process or production method' (emphasis added).

[10] See: G/TBT/1/Rev.15, pp 28–29. Confirmed in Panel Report, *US – Clove Cigarettes*, as anything above a *de minimis* level (paras 7.529–7.530).

situations in which a technical regulation *may* have a significant effect on trade of other Members'.[11] As a result, notification obligations under the TBT Agreement are construed widely, which has led some governments to err on the side of caution.[12]

Governments provide a set of information in their notifications, including:

- the lead government agency responsible for the measure (for example, legislation) within the notifying WTO Member and contact details;
- the products to which the measure relates;
- an overview of what the measure entails;
- its objective and rationale;
- the expected date of its entry into force; and
- the timeline for comments (usually 90 days).

Notifications now often include preliminary information about the need for such a measure within the section on its objective. In other words, it does not only say that it is intended to support public health policies, but it also justifies the use of *this specific measure* to pursue these objectives. Increasingly, Members reference evidence of the challenges they face and the basis of their measure – a positive evolution, as will be discussed in Chapter 5.

The way in which governments notify measures concerning technical barriers to trade is often more conservative than it needs to be. For example, where a new labelling measure is introduced, where the measure is aligned with an international standard (discussed in Chapter 6), the regulating Member

---

[11] Panel Report, *US – Clove Cigarettes* (DS406), paras 7.529–7.530 (emphasis in original).

[12] See, for example, the notification by the UK of the Food (Promotion and Placement) (England) Regulations 2021, which introduce placement and price promotion restrictions on unhealthy food in stores (both physical and online).

only needs to notify it and provide additional information if another Member requests it. However, it is common practice for some Members to notify *any* technical regulations that will have a significant impact on international trade to the TBT Committee. WTO Members act on the basis not only of their obligations but also of their *perceived* obligations.[13]

In practical terms, once a Member has decided that their (draft) measure should be notified, they will submit a notification to the WTO Secretariat. Some Members may wish to discuss this measure in more detail, and in a more public space. In these instances, they may include it on the agenda of the next committee meeting. This allows Members to raise any specific trade concerns regarding the measure: for example, it may be claimed that a labelling requirement mandating FoPNL or alcohol health warnings infringes the TBT Agreement because it is unnecessarily restrictive of trade, as we will discuss in Chapter 5. The notification procedure may therefore be a useful first step in resolving any potential disagreements before they escalate into a full-fledged legal dispute. Depending on the relevant legal commitments, other WTO bodies may be the focus – for example, where no other committee has a clear mandate, the Committee on Market Access will act as the relevant forum. And in some cases, Members may wish to raise the issue to a less technical and more political body (and thus 'escalate' matters) such as the Council for Trade in Goods.

Though this presents a very government-focused system, in practice, businesses – not least tobacco, alcohol, and food MNCs – have developed an extensive playbook of arguments, which they have invoked as part of the multifaceted lobbying strategies they use to protect their commercial interests. Although these arguments may not give an accurate depiction of what governments are required to do under WTO law, they

---

[13] This can be contrasted with other areas where Members are far less diligent, and indeed do not even meet the legal obligations they actually have, for example, for agricultural and industrial subsidies.

are nonetheless used extensively to put them under pressure to the point that they have, at times, abandoned or postponed the adoption or implementation of the contested measures. This is part of what is sometimes referred to as 'regulatory chill' – the restrictive influence of *perceived* obligations on governments under international economic law that are weaponized by businesses to protect their interests.

By the time a draft measure is notified to the WTO, it will (or should) have already gone through a detailed internal policy process, particularly as the playbook of the tobacco, alcohol, and food industries becomes increasingly well understood. Therefore, the regulating government *should* already be well prepared, having considered: the legitimacy of the objectives pursued; the existing evidence supporting a certain course of action; how tailored the presentation of the measure envisaged is to its specific objectives; and whether other measures could have offered a suitable alternative that would have been less trade-restrictive (as we will discuss in Chapter 5). In this regard, the notification process might be considered the first time that a measure is formally presented to the international community. However, affected businesses will already have been aware of the development of this measure, particularly those that operate across borders.[14] They will be prepared and have briefed other WTO Members where they have an economic presence, hoping they may be sympathetic and supportive of their concerns, and in a position to voice such concerns both formally at the Committee and informally before and after Committee meetings.

Therefore, the notification stage is an important step in the progress of the introduction of a trade-related public health measure. It also marks an important shift in how the justification of any measure must be framed in WTO-compatible language. Notifications often refer to a 'proportionate response', how business is given a 'very long lead-in time' to

---

[14] See the discussion in Chapter 1.

'minimize the impact on their processes'. All echo the core obligations resting on governments by virtue of WTO law, including predictability, non-discrimination, consistency, and necessity.

In the case of IP rights, the TRIPS Agreement (discussed in Chapter 7) also obliges Members to make certain notifications to the TRIPS Council. These notifications facilitate the Council's work of monitoring the operation of TRIPS and promote the transparency of Members' laws and policies on IP rights protection. Members wishing to avail themselves of certain flexibilities provided in TRIPS must also notify the Council.[15]

3.4 Regulatory cooperation: notifications and consultation under FTAs

The way in which the principle of predictability manifests itself in FTAs is similar, though with important differences. FTAs often go further than what we find under the WTO as they may also include provisions on regulatory cooperation, coherence, and good regulatory (or manufacturing) practices – in effect, enhanced notification and consultation obligations.

Some of these FTA commitments will build on what is already required under WTO law and go further. Such 'WTO+ commitments' are particularly common regarding notification and consultation on barriers to trade such as technical regulations. For example, under Article 8.7.13 CPTPP: 'A Party that publishes a notice and that files a notification in accordance with [the notification requirements] ... of the TBT Agreement or this Chapter shall: (a) include in the notification an explanation of the objectives of the proposal and how it would address those objectives.' CPTPP also requires the parties to provide greater detail in terms of

---

[15] Article 63.2 TRIPS.

justifying their technical regulation. For example, where a party receives a request, it must 'provide as soon as possible, but no later than 60 days after receiving a request from another Party, a description of alternative approaches, if any, that the Party considered in developing the final technical regulation or conformity assessment procedure and the merits of the approach that the Party selected'.[16]

In other FTAs, the obligations may go well beyond what we find at the WTO: these are known as 'WTO-X commitments'. For example, Article 18.6 of the EU–Japan Economic Partnership Agreement requires the parties to share information on *all* planned major regulatory measures annually. The Agreement also includes commitments to conduct impact assessments[17] of proposed major regulatory measures, and to ensure parties provide public consultations).[18] While these are good regulatory practice, they can be reframed by businesses (which may, for example, insist that they be consulted throughout the process) to stymie government action. This is not a necessary interpretation of these provisions, but as we have already noted, there is a gap between what the law requires and what it is presented by business interests as requiring. In such cases, governments can legitimately – and should – carefully review the text of their commitments and interpret them more narrowly than businesses often suggest.[19]

The purpose of these 'WTO+' and 'WTO-X' FTA commitments is to improve predictability for businesses and, in some cases, also to head off disputes before regulation becomes effective and disputes are harder to resolve. For example, the EU and the US have had decade-long trade disputes over regulatory approaches in several sectors, not least agri-food

---

[16] Article 8.7.18(b) CPTPP.
[17] Article 18.8.
[18] Article 18.7.
[19] Remembering also that the starting place is that states are only bound insofar as they have given their consent (see Chapter 2).

(for example, the hormone-treated beef dispute litigated at the WTO),[20] which are now so entrenched that they are hard to change. Regulatory cooperation chapters in FTAs are intended to encourage greater cooperation before measures enter into force, thus preventing such disputes from souring the wider bilateral relationship.

While this approach is laudable in many sectors, it presents challenges for public health regulation where Members have very different policies in place. Additionally, new measures on products such as tobacco, alcohol, or unhealthy food can be framed as trade-restrictive, as they increase costs (at least in the short term) for those specific industries, notwithstanding their critical public health objective or their wider economic benefits to society. Many FTA commitments include obligations to give industry actors additional access to consultations, require governments to show discredited alternatives to their proposed measure, and provide additional evidence and justification for it. Although, in isolation, these obligations are not particularly challenging and can be seen as good regulatory practices, together, where weaponized by businesses, they can be used to deter or undermine government regulation.[21] Regulatory cooperation may therefore need to be approached with caution.

As with notifications at the WTO, the process of notification and regulatory cooperation under FTAs should be factored into any regulatory process and strategic planning to anticipate, and successfully defend, challenges to new public health measures which may be met by resistance from within specific sectors, including the tobacco, alcohol, and food industries.

---

[20] For an illustrative selection, see WTO disputes DS26 (on beef hormones) and DS291 (on genetically modified products).

[21] 'Paralysis by analysis': see F de Ville and G Siles-Brügge 'Why TTIP Is a Game-Changer and Its Critics Have a Point', 24 *Journal of European Public Policy* 10 (2017) 1491.

3.5 Conclusions

Businesses like stability and predictability to minimize risk. When taking long-term economic decisions, changing regulatory environments can entail significant costs. Yet, governments are entitled to regulate to pursue public policy goals such as NCD prevention. Provided that they act in a reasonable manner, in line with their commitments under trade and investment agreements, such actions need not constitute an unpredictable change in behaviour (as also discussed in Chapter 8). Systems (of notifications) and obligations (of transition periods and legitimate expectations) do not restrict governments from acting to prevent NCDs. Rather, they require policy and regulatory processes that are designed with these considerations in mind, so that policy makers are prepared to respond to the push back they may receive from economic actors, and tobacco, alcohol, and food MNCs more specifically.

FOUR

The Principle of Non-Discrimination

4.1 Introduction

Free and fair competition is considered the best path to securing better-quality products at better prices for consumers, which in turn can contribute to an increase in economic development, greater prosperity, and improved health outcomes.[1] This is why the principle of non-discrimination is a core principle of the global economic order.

Non-discrimination takes two forms in international trade law, which this chapter discusses in turn:

- the prohibition of discriminating between products coming from different WTO Members ('MFN treatment'); and

---

[1] As noted in Chapter 2, the objective of the WTO is not an increase in trade by itself, but rather that trade policy 'should be conducted with a view to raising standards of living, ensuring full employment and a large and steadily growing volume of real income and effective demand, and expanding the production of and trade in goods and services, while allowing for the optimal use of the world's resources in accordance with the objective of sustainable development' (WTO Agreement, Preamble, 1st recital).

- the prohibition of discrimination between domestic and imported products ('national treatment').

For our purposes, it is important to bear in mind that non-discrimination plays an important role in both the design and the implementation of the measures that governments may want to introduce to prevent NCDs. Where these measures favour domestic over foreign traders of tobacco, alcohol, or food *by virtue of the origin of these goods*, this is likely to give rise to serious concerns under international trade law.

4.2 Most-favoured nation treatment

The MFN obligation is considered a pillar of the multilateral trading system. Under Article I.1 GATT:

> With respect to customs duties and charges of any kind imposed on or in connection with importation or exportation … any advantage, favour, privilege or immunity granted by any contracting party to any product originating in or destined for any other country shall be accorded immediately and unconditionally to the like product originating in or destined for the territories of all other contracting parties.

In short, Article I GATT requires WTO Members to grant any benefit they confer on the goods of one Member to like products of another Member, immediately and unconditionally.[2] These benefits often consist of lower tariffs. However, the concept of a 'benefit' is defined widely to include 'any advantage, favour, privilege or immunity', thus covering the treatment of products at a border.[3] MFN therefore aims to

---

[2] A comparable provision exists under the GATS in services: Article II GATS.

[3] For example, *Colombia – Ports of Entry* (DS366).

avoid discrimination between Members and 'multilateralize' any concessions that WTO Members give. To this effect, it prohibits one WTO Member from granting preferential access to their market over another.

This is subject to an important caveat: equivalent treatment does not have to be given to *all* products – only those that are 'like'. Likeness is a central concept of international trade law and is fundamentally linked to competition in the marketplace: where products are alike, they should be in some form of competitive relationship, hence the reason why the law seeks to minimize the ability of governments to distort competition between them. The exact interpretation of likeness depends on the specific legal provision in question in each case, but there are some general rules which can be identified.[4]

4.2.1 What are 'like products'?

If two products are so different that they are neither alike nor in a competitive relationship (for example, apples and armchairs), differences in how these products are treated cannot amount to discrimination for the purposes of international trade law. In other words, a comparator is necessary to compare goods meaningfully.

Apples and apples are clearly alike to the extent that they are the same product type. However, does this mean that they are necessarily 'like products' for the purposes of WTO law? There are several apple varieties (Granny Smith, Braeburn, Gala, Cox, Pink Lady, and so on), many of which have different uses: some are used for cooking, others for eating raw and so on. This raises the question of whether and, if so, how they should be distinguished.

WTO panels and the Appellate Body have provided extensive guidance on how to determine 'likeness'. When examining

---

[4] As we will examine further later on, 'likeness' is understood differently under Articles I, III.2 and III.4 GATT.

whether products are 'like products' for the purposes of MFN, the first set of relevant criteria are the 'Border Tax Adjustment' criteria, named after an early GATT-era dispute.[5] These criteria are: physical properties, end use, consumer tastes, and tariff classifications. Though useful, they are not always sufficient to determine 'likeness'. The case law has therefore evolved to focus on the existence of a competitive relationship. This is logical: if the purpose of the rule is to avoid the distortion of competition between products, the existence of a competitive relationship is key.[6] A consequence of this development is that the answer whether goods are 'like' will depend on each market, potentially requiring extensive and complex market analysis to determine substitutability.

4.2.2 The implications of the MFN obligation for public health policy

The most common application of MFN relates to tariffs. As noted in Chapter 3, Members can choose to apply either the highest possible tariff they can adopt in the absence of a specific exception (the 'bound' rate) or a lower tariff ('applied' rate). However, if they choose the lower tariff, WTO law requires that they proceed on an MFN basis: the lower tariff must be equally granted to the like products of all trading partners.

In case of tobacco, alcohol, or unhealthy food, the choice of tariff can present serious challenges, as the case of Samoa's accession to the WTO discussed in Chapter 3 demonstrates. By virtue of the MFN obligation, WTO law is clear that where a tariff is reduced, it cannot be limited only to a small, limited number of countries. There are exceptions to

---

[5]   'Border Tax Adjustments', Report of the Working Party adopted on 2 December 1970 (L/3464).

[6]   For an overview of the different approaches taken in the case law, see Panel Report, *US – Poultry (China)* (DS392), paras 7.424–7.426.

this rule (including the conclusion of FTAs), but in relation to multilateral tariff reductions, as large exporters in other markets will also have to be granted similar access, this creates a multiplier effect of the potential harm to human health. Where such commodities are concerned, WTO Members may therefore need to tread carefully when determining their 'bound' rate and when potentially lowering their applied rate.

4.2.3 MFN treatment and FTAs

Notwithstanding the MFN obligation, WTO Members give preferential market access to some Members over others, principally by concluding FTAs between a limited set of partners.[7] As mentioned earlier, under FTAs, the parties agree to liberalize further than they have done at the WTO ('WTO+ commitments') and often include additional commitments that do not (yet) exist at the WTO – for example, on labour rights or climate action ('WTO-X commitments').

As FTAs allow parties to give each other preferential access beyond that which they offer all other WTO Members, they must meet specific legal requirements set out under Article XXIV GATT to justify what would otherwise be a violation of the MFN obligation.[8] Specifically, FTA partners must, inter alia, liberalize 'substantially all the trade' between the parties.[9] This is the bargain contained in the trade regime: either engage in non-discriminatory multilateral trade or liberalize sufficiently among FTA partners so that the price of discrimination in the

---

[7] Another exception to MFN exists under the 'Enabling Clause', which permits granting unilateral tariff preferences for developing countries (commonly referred to as a Generalized System of Preferences or GSP). The impact of GSP programmes is of limited relevance for NCD prevention and so we have chosen to prioritize discussion of FTAs here.

[8] A parallel provision exists in services: Article V GATS.

[9] There is very little case law on this provision to date. Limited guidance is presented in the Appellate Body Report of *Turkey – Textiles* (DS34).

system is acceptable to all. As improved market access is the rule under WTO law, including for tobacco, alcohol, and unhealthy food, FTA negotiating partners have little discretion to limit those tariff commitments. Furthermore, in trade relations, power comes from market size. Therefore, when large players such as the US or the EU negotiate FTAs with smaller partners, the latter rarely have the ability to exclude products from liberalization. This explains, at least in part, why when governments decide to act to prevent NCDs, they prioritize regulation or taxation over tariffs.

4.3 National treatment

Another pillar of the multilateral trading system is the 'national treatment' obligation: the obligation not to treat imported products less favourably than domestic products based on the origin of the goods.[10] In effect, while the MFN obligation prohibits discrimination between 'like' products that are imported from different countries, the national treatment obligation prohibits discrimination between domestic and imported products.

The national treatment obligation applies to a wide range of government measures, many of which will be relevant to the prevention of NCDs. These include:

- internal taxes: indirect sales tax, such as excise duties and value-added tax (VAT); and
- mandatory regulations covering a wide variety of rules on how products are made, packaged, labelled, and marketed, including bans on the sale of products.

National treatment commitments are found in several provisions of WTO law.

---

[10] Article III GATT and later, in a different way, Article 2.2 of the TBT Agreement.

Table 4.1: National treatment provisions under WTO law

Provision	Commitment
Article III.2 GATT	Prohibition of discrimination on 'internal taxes or other internal charges of any kind'[11]
Article III.4 GATT	Prohibition of discrimination on 'all laws, regulations and requirements affecting the internal sale, offering for sale, purchase, transportation, distribution or use' of 'like products'
Article 2.1 TBT Agreement	National treatment for technical regulations[12]
Article 3 TRIPS Agreement	National treatment for protection of IP[13]

It is also common for FTAs to either replicate the language of Article III GATT and/or Article 2.1 of the TBT Agreement in their text, or to incorporate them by reference.

As Table 4.1 shows, national treatment manifests itself in different legal commitments. While the precise application and interpretation of these commitments varies depending on the wording, case law, and context, we can synthesize the core elements from a public health perspective. The US ban on clove cigarettes illustrates how the non-discrimination operates

---

[11] As will be discussed later on, the rigour of the national treatment obligation under Article III.2 depends upon the relationship between the products in question: the more similar they are, the stricter the rules.

[12] A technical regulation is defined in Annex 1(1) of the TBT Agreement as a '[d]ocument which lays down product characteristics or their related processes and production methods, including the applicable administrative provisions, with which compliance is mandatory. It may also include or deal exclusively with terminology, symbols, packaging, marking or labelling requirements as they apply to a product, process or production method'.

[13] See further Chapter 7.

when governments introduce NCD prevention measures in violation of their national treatment obligation.[14]

Prohibiting discriminatory regulation: US – Clove Cigarettes

In 2009, the US adopted the Family Smoking Prevention Tobacco Control Act, which was intended to reduce smoking, especially among young people. To this effect, it banned clove and other flavoured cigarettes, as young people were more likely to start smoking flavoured tobacco that masked the harshness of tobacco. Most forms of flavoured tobacco were banned. However, the prohibition did not apply to menthol cigarettes.

In 2010, Indonesia, the principal producer and exporter of clove cigarettes to the US, challenged this measure, arguing that the US had discriminated between imported clove cigarettes and 'like' domestically produced menthol cigarettes, and was therefore incompatible with Article 2.1 of the TBT Agreement. Both the WTO Panel and the Appellate Body found that clove and menthol cigarettes were in a competitive relationship (they were 'like products') and that, by giving preferential treatment to goods originated within its borders (menthol cigarettes) to the detriment of imported goods (clove cigarettes), the US had indeed violated the national treatment obligation. Importantly, this was the case even though the measure did not explicitly refer to any differential treatment between imported and home-produced cigarettes.

It is crucial to note that the conclusion of the dispute was not that the US could not ban clove cigarettes; rather, it was that if it was to ban clove cigarettes, it had to ban other like products to meet its WTO obligations, namely all other flavoured tobacco products in a competitive relationship with clove cigarettes, including menthol cigarettes.

However, the political realities of passing legislation that harmed large menthol producers in the US made this unlikely. It is telling that while the US was required to either ban both cloves and menthols or neither, it took a third way following the dispute. In 2014, Indonesia and the US reached a settlement (a 'mutually agreed solution'), whereby the US agreed:

---

[14]   *US – Clove Cigarettes* (DS406).

- to provide Indonesia with preferential access on certain other goods;
- not to sue Indonesia over other noncompliant WTO measures it maintained; and
- to hold dialogues on more effective IP rights protection in Indonesia.

On 24 January 2025, the Trump administration withdrew the plan to ban menthol cigarettes and flavoured cigars which the Federal Drugs Administration (FDA) had proposed in April 2022 and finalised in October 2023.

The taxation regime of alcoholic beverages presents another interesting example, as it is common practice for governments to tax stronger alcoholic beverages at a higher rate. We use a hypothetical example to consider how the principle of non-discrimination and national treatment operates.

Let us assume that WTO Member Alpha's tax code sets out the following sales tax given in Table 4.2 for alcoholic beverages based on their alcohol by volume (ABV).

Table 4.2: Hypothetical example of a table on alcoholic beverages taxation

Product	Strength (alcohol by volume)	Tax per litre
Beer (lager)	1.2–2.8%	5 pence
	2.8–7.5%	10 pence
	More than 7.5%	15 pence
Beer (wheat beer)	1.2–2.8%	10 pence
	2.8–7.5%	20 pence
	More than 7.5%	30 pence
Cider	1.2–2.8%	10 pence
	2.8–7.5%	20 pence
	More than 7.5%	30 pence

Alpha produces 90 per cent of the lager that is consumed domestically. Wheat beer is mostly imported from WTO Member Beta, while WTO Member Gamma produces cider. Wheat beer and cider producers are unhappy that their products are subject to a higher tax. They have lobbied their governments successfully to raise their specific trade concerns with Alpha. For its part, Alpha considers that its tax regime is reasonable and claims that there are at least two good reasons to discourage the consumption of wheat beer and cider: (1) to support local businesses; and (2) to discourage the consumption of higher calorie beverages. It also defends its taxation system by arguing that lager, wheat beer, and cider are so different from each other that their different treatment does not equate to discrimination under WTO law. By contrast, Beta and Gamma respond that wheat beer and cider clearly are in a competitive relationship with Alpha's lager and that therefore the lack of equality of competitive opportunities between them infringes the national treatment obligation.

Ultimately, to know which is right, it is necessary to answer a series of questions:

- whether the products that are being compared are alike for the purposes of WTO law;
- whether Alpha has discriminated against imported goods for the purposes of WTO law; and
- whether the less favourable treatment imposed on imported goods may be justified by a legitimate reason of public interest rather than the origin of the goods itself.

We consider these three questions in turn.

4.3.1 A broad understanding of 'like products': similar goods in competition

We noted previously that an assessment of likeness would usually start with the 'border tax adjustment' criteria: physical properties, end use, consumer tastes, and tariff classifications. An important difference between the national treatment obligation under Article III GATT and the one found in Article I GATT (MFN) is that a provision of Article III prohibits discrimination between both 'like products' and products that are 'directly competitive or substitutable'.[15] Specifically, while Article III.4 on national treatment in respect of domestic regulation only refers to 'like' products, Article III.2 on national treatment in respect of *taxation* includes reference to two categories of goods in competition: 'like' products and 'directly competitive or substitutable' products. For lawyers, this difference has had to be explained, interpreted, and applied. For our purposes, the key consequence is that the more alike two products are, the stricter the test for discrimination.

For example, two products which are almost identical (for example, Spanish and Italian lemons) can be subjected to no difference in taxation, even by the smallest amount. By contrast, products which are competitive but not entirely alike – technically, 'directly competitive or substitutable' products – cannot be taxed in such a way 'as to afford protection to domestic production'.[16] This could mean a slight difference in taxation is permissible for the latter, while it is not for the former. The logic behind this interpretation of the provisions of Article III GATT is that if we are concerned about non-discrimination, the more similar the products are, the stricter the rule if we are to ensure fair competition and trading conditions. It is ultimately a question of degree and therefore depends on assessment of the specific facts for each case.

---

[15] Article III GATT. There is considerable case law and literature on the exact interpretation of likeness under Article III GATT. For a detailed account of the development of the case law, see H Hestermeyer, 'Article III GATT', in G Messenger (ed), *Commentaries of World Trade Law: Volume 2, Trade in Goods* (Leiden: Brill, 2nd edn, 2025).

[16] An explanation of the law can be found in the Appellate Body's reasoning in *Japan – Alcoholic Beverages* (DS8/10/11), p 24.

Returning to Alpha, the question of whether wheat beer and cider are 'like products' is key. If they are, then Alpha cannot apply higher taxes to some of them but not others. At the other hand of the spectrum, if lager, wheat beer, and cider are neither 'like products' nor 'directly competitive or substitutable', then Alpha is free to tax these products as it wishes, as there can be no discrimination. Finally, if lager, wheat beer, and cider are 'directly competitive or substitutable', then Alpha cannot tax these products in such a way as to afford protection to its domestic production of lager to the detriment of imported wheat beer and cider.

How would we determine if these products are 'like products' or 'directly competitive or substitutable products'? One may wonder whether the differences between the products at stake here prevent them from being considered 'like products' or 'directly competitive or substitutable' products. In particular, they use different ingredients as their base, which make their physical characteristics fundamentally different, likely preventing these three products from being considered sufficiently similar to be classified as 'like products' in the narrower sense of the term. They also have different tariff classifications. That said, they are consumed in similar circumstances and therefore satisfy similar consumer purposes. They also go through similar processes (that is, fermentation, not distillation). As such, while they are unlikely to be 'like', they may still be sufficiently closely related in the market to be considered 'directly competitive or substitutable'. To assess this, we would need to determine whether consumers would see them as substitutable for each other and, in particular, if the price of one was to go up, would they switch to the other? To answer this question, we would need to engage in market analysis and assess cross-price elasticity.[17] These assessments will be market-specific as

---

[17] Cross-price elasticity = % change in price of good B%/change in quantity demanded of good A.

consumer behaviour is different across markets and often require extensive and, at times, extremely complex economic analysis.

4.3.2 A broad understanding of the notion of 'discrimination': discrimination in law and discrimination in fact

The notion of discrimination has been interpreted widely by WTO panels and the Appellate Body. First, it covers direct discrimination, that is, instances of explicit discrimination, where WTO Members adopt measures that, on their face, put goods coming from other WTO Members at a disadvantage. Such measures are discriminatory both in law and in fact. This would be the case, for example, if Alpha subjected the importation of alcoholic beverages from Beta or Gamma to a tax not payable by similar alcoholic beverages produced within its borders. Direct discrimination may also arise because the imported products are taxed at a higher rate than similar domestic products or because the host Member State uses different methods for calculating the tax for domestic and imported goods to the disadvantage of the latter.

Second, the notion of discrimination also covers measures that are indirectly discriminatory – that is, measures which do not refer to nationality on their face (in law) but nonetheless have a discriminatory effect on goods originating from other Member states (in fact). This was the case in the *US – Clove Cigarettes* dispute mentioned earlier: the US legislation did not specifically refer to the origin of the goods (for example, the US for menthols or Indonesia for cloves), although the exemption of menthols from its scope was clearly intended to protect the home market, thus granting a competitive advantage to US flavoured cigarette manufacturers over foreign (and particularly Indonesian) competitors.[18]

---

[18] *US – Clove Cigarettes* (DS406). The paradigmatic example of this in relation to taxation is *Japan – Alcoholic Beverages* (DS8/10/11), where the government structured the internal taxation system to protect local shochu producers.

Similarly, in our hypothetical example, Alpha claimed that it had good reasons to discourage the consumption of wheat beer and cider, including supporting local businesses and discouraging the consumption of higher calorie beverages. This raises the next question: the extent to which WTO rules allow Members to differentiate between products to pursue legitimate public policy objectives, including public health protection. Here again, we will emphasize the importance of ensuring that governments do not invoke these objectives to mask discriminatory policies.

4.3.3 Non-discrimination as a condition of public policy exceptions

A government may pursue certain public interest objectives, such as the protection of public health, which may justify the use of a taxation/regulatory scheme that would otherwise fall foul of the national treatment obligation under WTO law. However, governments must tread carefully and ensure that the measures they adopt cannot be construed as pursing a protectionist agenda rather than the legitimate objectives they claim to pursue.

In our example, Alpha indicated that its taxation scheme aimed to discourage the consumption of higher calorie beverages by increasing their price through taxation. Alpha could also have invoked other legitimate objectives, not least the prevention of alcohol-related harm. However, Alpha's acknowledgement that it had taxed specific beverages to discourage consumption of the imported beverages and therefore afford preferential treatment to home-produced beverages is particularly problematic: any overt or covert attempt at shielding the home market from foreign competition is simply unacceptable under WTO law. Legitimate objectives may not be coupled with preferential treatment of one's own products.

As mentioned earlier, non-discrimination commitments relevant to the prevention of NCDs principally come into

WTO law through three different instruments: the GATT, the TBT Agreement, and the TRIPS Agreement. However, the structure of these different instruments is somewhat different, which has an impact on how WTO Members can rely on the pursuit of an objective such as protecting human health as a 'defence' where they have otherwise violated their WTO obligations. For example, under the TBT Agreement, there is no explicit 'exception' provision that can be relied upon as a defence if a measure violates another provision of the TBT Agreement. Instead, the analysis focuses on the extent to which there is a 'legitimate regulatory distinction' between the products in question.[19]

Under the GATT, there is a specific exception provision that governments can rely on where their policy would otherwise violate the GATT. Article XX GATT sets out a list of public policy aims that are covered – which comprise public morals (Article XX(a)), human health (Article XX(b)), and exhaustible natural resources (Article XX(g)), including clean air.[20]

To avoid WTO Members abusing Article XX GATT to justify measures that would otherwise not be permissible, the introductory provision to Article XX, known as the *chapeau*, provides as follows:

> Subject to the requirement that such measures are not applied in a manner which would constitute a means of arbitrary or unjustifiable discrimination between countries where the same conditions prevail, or a disguised restriction on international trade, nothing in this Agreement shall be construed to prevent the adoption or enforcement by any contracting party of measures

After which it lists (inter alia) those 'necessary to protect human, animal or plant life or health'.

---

[19] Appellate Body Report, *US – Tuna II (Mexico)* (DS381), para 216.

[20] For example, *US – Gasoline* (DS2).

There are other components of any defence, not least the necessity of the measure that will be discussed in Chapter 5. We nonetheless already see the centrality of the non-discrimination principle throughout the policy cycle. WTO Members cannot discriminate when implementing NCD prevention measures, and they will not be able to defend such measures from legal challenges if they are indeed discriminatory and do not rest of a legitimate objective.

In designing NCD prevention measures, governments must ensure that these measures do not discriminate (1) between like domestic and imported products; and (2) between different foreign products. Moreover, *should* there be discrimination, it cannot be 'unjustifiable', but must result instead from a 'legitimate' reason to distinguish between the regulation of the products. The bar is understandably high, but, from an NCD prevention perspective, potentially beneficial, as a carefully designed measure which may be discriminatory for reasons other than the origin of the goods may contribute to better health outcomes.

4.4 Conclusion

The principle of non-discrimination is central in international economic law. This chapter has focused on its relevance to WTO law, while Chapter 8 considers its relevance in international investment law. When governments regulate to protect public health or other interests, they cannot do so in a way which disadvantages foreign producers or investors. Insisting throughout the policy process on a more comprehensive measure that does not discriminate in favour of selected domestic economic interests can, ultimately, produce more effective public health outcomes than partial measures, as the *US – Clove Cigarettes* dispute demonstrates. These measures are also more defensible under international trade and investment law. When faced with arguments from specific business sectors, governments need to hold the principle of non-discrimination at the forefront of their mind throughout the policy process. However, once this principle is clearly understood, it is arguably far easier to implement than the principle of necessity, to which we will turn next.

FIVE

The Principle of Necessity

5.1 Introduction

A primary preoccupation of the trade regime is to ensure that governments do not unduly restrict trade in the course of their activities. However, it also recognizes that governments need to protect public health and other legitimate interests in ways that can affect international trade. This is why a core set of obligations in international trade law relate to the principle of 'necessity', sometimes also referred to as 'proportionality'. This principle requires that when governments act, they should do so in a targeted manner, so that such activity is designed to achieve the specific objectives it pursues while considering its impact on other interests. To this end, governments are required to develop laws and regulations in light of the relevant evidence, and tailor such laws and regulations to the objectives they pursue. An important part of the necessity assessment therefore entails that governments identify the relevant evidence on which their laws and policies rest, and determine how such evidence base can help them achieve a complex balance between these potentially competing interests.

As with non-discrimination, the necessity principle cuts across multiple legal obligations under various WTO agreements, not least the GATT and the TBT Agreement.

As noted in Chapter 4, the different legal provisions have consequences in terms of how they function. The GATT contains obligations and a set of 'general exceptions', which includes the protection of health (Article XX(b)) and on which Members can rely to justify measures that would otherwise be in violation of GATT obligations. Meanwhile, under the TBT Agreement, in the absence of a provision containing an explicit exception, the obligations have been interpreted to include a built-in exception where the difference in treatment between goods stems from a 'legitimate regulatory distinction'.[1]

The concepts of 'necessity' and 'proportionality' are loaded with meaning for lawyers, often subject to vast amounts of elaborate case law and doctrinal analysis. However, for the purposes of this short book, we have sought to distil the underlying logic of these obligations with a view to identifying how they shape government measures, particularly those intended to prevent NCDs. While the concepts of 'necessity' and 'proportionality' are comparatively clear, they can be difficult to apply in practice, as they are contingent on the specific laws and policies adopted in a given country, based on specific factual circumstances and the underpinning evidence.

In the international trade context, the need to notify WTO Members of specific new measures ahead of their implementation, especially technical regulations, was discussed in Chapter 3. New public health measures will often be accompanied by reference to a relevant evidence base with a view to justifying these measures. Such engagement with evidence is an important part of the process, particularly in order to prevent challenges from trading partners at an early stage. This is even more so as necessity challenges are some of the most commonly invoked against NCD prevention measures.

As will be discussed in Chapter 8, this practice of engaging early on with underpinning evidence is also relevant in the investment context. However, in this chapter, we focus on

---

[1]   Appellate Body Report, *US – Clove Cigarettes* (DS406), para 174.

WTO law and, more specifically, the lessons that can be learned from the interpretation of the TBT Agreement (section 5.2) and the GATT (section 5.3), and the role of evidence in defending NCD prevention measures (section 5.4). Finally, we briefly consider FTAs (section 5.5), before concluding (section 5.6).

5.2 Tailoring measures to their objectives

A central obligation under the TBT Agreement is that any mandatory rules that relate to how products are made or how they are to look – that is, any technical regulations – 'shall not be more trade-restrictive than necessary to fulfil a legitimate objective, taking account of the risks non-fulfilment would create', as per Article 2.2 of the TBT Agreement. In other words, measures can be trade-restrictive but not 'unnecessarily trade-restrictive'. This recognizes the imperative for WTO law to accommodate other interests than trade, including public health protection.

Article 2.2 of the TBT Agreement

Members shall ensure that technical regulations are not prepared, adopted or applied with a view to or with the effect of creating unnecessary obstacles to international trade. For this purpose, technical regulations shall not be more trade-restrictive than necessary to fulfil a legitimate objective, taking account of the risks non-fulfilment would create. Such legitimate objectives are, inter alia: national security requirements; the prevention of deceptive practices; protection of human health or safety, animal or plant life or health, or the environment. In assessing such risks, relevant elements of consideration are, inter alia: available scientific and technical information, related processing technology or intended end-uses of products.

Labelling requirements provide a helpful example. They may constitute barriers to trade, as they can add costs for producers that may require the creation of new production lines or packaging facilities for a specific market and therefore could make their products less competitive in this market. Certain labelling requirements may also reduce trade – for example, when a government imposes tobacco plain packaging, alcohol health warnings or FoPNL to discourage consumption. Therefore, the question for governments is to determine how they can restrict trade as part of their NCD prevention strategies without doing so 'unnecessarily', which would be incompatible with Article 2.2 of the TBT Agreement.

Determining whether a measure is necessary in this context requires that we answer several questions, which are all part of the 'necessity test' and open different avenues for legal challenges:

- First, whether the measure pursues one or several legitimate objectives, and whether it is likely to achieve these objectives. Defining the objective in light of existing evidence is key to assessing legitimacy.
- Second, whether there may be alternative measures that would allow a given state to achieve the objectives pursued while being less restrictive of trade. Often, industry actors have suggested that providing consumer education and information could be less restrictive of trade than regulating product composition, labelling, packaging, and marketing. However, these arguments have serious shortcomings, in that they ignore the crucial fact that information and education campaigns are no substitute for marketing restrictions; they are complementary and must work together to promote healthier environments.

The requirement that a measure be no more 'trade-restrictive than necessary' to fulfil its legitimate objective(s) is challenging, and is one of the most common questions put to governments at the WTO TBT Committee.[2] Whereas accusations of discrimination can be addressed by demonstrating that no

---

[2] Data from 'Navigating Trade Challenge at the World Trade Organization to Prevent Non-Communicable Diseases and Promote Better Health for All' (NIHR204663).

competitive relationship exists between imported and domestic products, it is harder to counter the claim that any number of hypothetical alternatives might be preferable. Fortunately, the interpretation of this obligation has been expanded to allow governments more freedom to determine both how far they want to prevent NCDs and the means they deploy to this effect.

The *Australia – Tobacco Plain Packaging* dispute has become emblematic of how public health and trade interests may collide and be reconciled to promote better health for all. While tobacco measures had been litigated under trade law previously,[3] this dispute marked the culmination of significant transnational lobbying and campaigning from the tobacco industry, and diligent work by the public health community. The dispute was complex and touched on a wide range of issues concerning the relationship between NCD prevention and international trade law. We focus on necessity in the following section, while other issues are discussed in subsequent chapters.

Balancing interests: Australia – Tobacco Plain Packaging (DS435, 441, 458 and 467)

Australia developed a comprehensive set of restrictions on retail packaging of tobacco, including through the imposition of 'tobacco plain packaging' (TPP). It introduced its legislation in 2011: the Tobacco Plain Packaging Act 2011 (No 148, 2011) – 'An Act to discourage the use of tobacco products, and for related purposes'. More specifically, the aims of TPP were set out as follows:

(a) Tobacco plain packaging is intended to: (i) reduce the appeal of tobacco products to consumers; (ii) increase the effectiveness of the health warnings; and (iii) reduce the ability of the packaging to mislead consumers about the harmful effects of smoking.

---

[3] A GATT dispute, *Thailand – Restrictions on the Importation of and Internal Taxes on Cigarettes* (DS10R), and WTO disputes *Dominican Republic – Import and Sale of Cigarettes* (DS302) and *Thailand – Cigarettes* (the Philippines) (DS371), which were principally concerned with customs formalities, and *US – Clove Cigarettes* (DS406), as discussed in Chapter 4.

(b) If the TPP measures operate as intended upon any one or any combination of the above three mechanisms, then Australian consumers are expected to be discouraged from taking up smoking (initiation) or resuming smoking (relapse), and to be encouraged to stop smoking (cessation) and reduce exposure to second-hand smoke.

(c) As a consequence, positive public health outcomes – specifically reduced use of, and exposure to, tobacco products, and an associated reduction in tobacco-related disease and deaths – would arise.[4]

Cuba, the Dominican Republic, Honduras, and Indonesia – which were prepared to represent the interests of tobacco MNCs – challenged the measure on a range of grounds. In particular, they claimed that TPP was more trade-restrictive than it needed to be to meet Australia's stated objectives. Formal consultations – the first step in a legal dispute – were requested in 2012, the year after the legislation was passed. It took two years for the panel to be composed and a further four years for the panel report to be finalized and circulated. Following an appeal, the Appellate Body report was circulated on 9 June 2020, some nine years after the adoption of the relevant legislation.

The Appellate Body found that these TPP measures would make a meaningful contribution to Australia's objective of improving public health and that the complainants had failed to demonstrate that they were more trade-restrictive than necessary to fulfil this legitimate objective. The Appellate Body stressed the importance of taking into account the nature and gravity of the risks that would arise if Australia did not meet its objectives.

While the complainants had proposed other alternative measures, none of these were less trade-restrictive than TPP, which, in part, showed that Australia had considered a range of reasonable alternatives and tailored these measures to its objective. The argument that Australia's TPP measures were more trade-restrictive than was necessary was therefore rejected.[5]

---

[4] Appellate Body Report, *Australia - Tobacco Plain Packaging* (DS435), pp 34–35.

[5] For an introduction to *Australia – Tobacco Plain Packaging*, see also A Mitchell, *Tobacco Plain Packaging in Australia: Implications of the WTO Disputes* (Geneva: WHO, 2022).

The question over *exactly* how tailored a measure is to prevent NCDs, and what alternatives are available, is a difficult one for WTO Members to address if they are not confident in their position. We will remind readers that it is not only in litigation that measures have be defended, but also in informal discussions, FTA committees and joint bodies, and WTO committees.

We cannot exhaustively discuss the 800+-page decision of the panel and the 200+-page decision of the Appellate Body in the *Australia – Tobacco Plain Packaging* dispute. We therefore highlight four key points stemming from the dispute that WTO Members and the public health community at large should very much keep at the forefront of their minds. However, one thing is clear: if a government is uncertain as to whether the measures it envisages are 'necessary' for the purposes of Article 2.2 of the TBT Agreement, it would be well advised to liaise with a legal team with expertise in international trade law in order to frame the existing evidence supporting these measures in light of the relevant legal tests that apply. And the sooner this can be done – ideally from the pre-notification stage, the more likely the given measure(s) can withstand 'necessity' challenges.

First, the proposed or applied measure does not need to fully achieve, on its own, the policy objective(s) pursued. This is often impossible, as regulatory problems are rarely simple. In this respect, the case of NCD prevention is paradigmatic: it is well established that 'there is no silver [or magic] bullet' and that only multi-faceted, whole-of-government approaches are likely to effectively prevent NCDs. The law recognizes this complexity, requiring only that a measure contribute to the objective(s) pursued. The level of contribution the measure makes to a legitimate objective, and the risks of not acting, is weighed against the trade-restrictiveness of the measure.[6] Put

---

[6]   Appellate Body Report, *US – Tuna II (Mexico)* (DS381), para 318.

simply, the greater the contribution of the measure(s) adopted to achieve the objective(s), the more leeway Members have. However, this does *not* mean that Members are unable to act where the contribution of the measure(s) to the objective(s) is limited.

Second, how WTO Members identify and present the legitimate objective they pursue is important and requires careful strategic thinking on their part. It should be noted that while there are benefits to be more specific regarding the objective of the measure to better evidence the contribution that a measure may make to it, it does not need to be excluded from a wider NCD prevention or public health policy position. For example, in the recent *EU – Palm Oil (Malaysia)* dispute, the Panel explicitly noted that the objective of the EU measure in question was to reduce greenhouse gas emissions from indirect land use change associated with crop-based biofuels. However:

> [This] relatively narrow and direct formulation of the objective of the specific measures at issue can be understood not as an end in and of itself, but as a means towards fulfilling the higher-level objective of mitigating the climate crisis, which may in turn be understood as a means to fulfilling further higher-level objectives relating to the consequences of the climate crisis on the planet and human, animal or plant life or health.[7]

This ruling is important from a public health perspective as it recognizes the challenges that governments will unavoidably face when addressing complex societal problems such as NCD prevention. As is discussed throughout this book, these problems unavoidably require governments to address, as consistently and comprehensively as possible, all the causal

---

[7] Panel Report, *EU and Certain Member States – Palm Oil (Malaysia)* (DS600), para 7.220.

factors (both immediate and more structural) that underpin tobacco, alcohol, and unhealthy food consumption. This, in turn, invites us to reflect on how objectives can be strategically presented by governments at the WTO and other forums where their policies may be challenged on the ground that the relationship between the objectives they pursue and the means they deploy to achieve these objectives is not sufficiently established. The overall objective of their NCD prevention strategies will naturally be to prevent NCDs at the population level by, in particular, reducing the consumption of tobacco, alcohol, and unhealthy food, while increasing the consumption of healthy food. However, it is difficult to demonstrate that individual measures which are likely to be challenged by the tobacco, alcohol, and food industries on international trade and other legal grounds reduce NCDs, although they contribute to this objective and are, as such, an important component of these strategies.[8]

These evidential problems are exacerbated because effective NCD prevention strategies require the implementation of measures aimed at influencing consumer demand (not merely supply), which rests on both rational and less rational elements. Such difficulties are further compounded by the fact that demand reduction measures are still, in relative terms, in their infancy and their effectiveness has not always been quantified.[9] Unsurprisingly, the tobacco, alcohol, and food industries have extensively used these difficulties in litigation, trying to convince courts and tribunals that the measures were not 'necessary' or were 'disproportionate' to achieve the objective of

---

[8] For a discussion of how governments can strengthen their legal positions when developing and implementing food marketing restrictions to protect children from its harmful impact, see the UNICEF-WHO Toolkit on *Taking Action to Protect Children from the Harmful Impact of Food Marketing: A Child Rights-Based Approach* (Geneva: WHO and UNICEF, 2023).

[9] M Melillo, *Weaponising Evidence: A History of Tobacco Control in International Law* (Cambridge: Cambridge University Press, 2024), p 204.

preventing NCDs. Consequently, there is a strategic advantage to framing the objectives pursued more narrowly so that the challenged government (at the WTO or elsewhere) can more easily adduce evidence supporting the specific claims underpinning individual measures that will often form the package of measures supporting broader NCD prevention strategies. For example, when adopting a FoPNL scheme such as a warning label, a government is on a stronger footing if it states that the objectives it pursues are to better inform consumers of the risks involved in consuming large amounts of food high in calories, fat, sugar, or salt, to disincentivize such consumption, to improve diets, and ultimately to contribute to the prevention of diet-related NCDs and better health for all.

Third, the 'weighing and balancing' process considers the importance of the objective of the government as it regulates. This is key and has been interpreted to mean that the measure and its impact on the goal is balanced with the importance of the objective and the consequences of not meeting the government's aims. From an NCD perspective, where the objective is to improve public health, expressed narrowly through specific objectives such as improving consumer awareness of the nutritional content of products, this tips the scales (somewhat) in favour of the regulating government.

Fourth, once the regulating government has explained its position, it is for the challenging government(s) to show that a 'better' (that is, less trade-restrictive) measure is reasonably available.[10] There are two important points to make in this respect. First, the alternative measure identified needs to be 'reasonably available'. This demonstrates that the case law acknowledges the regulatory capacity of the challenged government. Second, the alternative measure identified must be a genuine 'alternative'. This is particularly relevant for NCD prevention policies, as claims are often put forward by industry

---

[10] This is a question of where the burden of proof lies. On this point, see further, section 5.3.

and supporting governments that public information or school education campaigns should be envisaged as alternatives to regulatory measures. Such claims omit to consider the core point that policy measures will often be cumulative – each contributing to an effective NCD prevention agenda in their own right – rather than 'alternative'. The necessity test therefore requires the identification of one or more alternative measures that should be both as effective as the contested one and less trade-restrictive to achieve the objective(s) pursued. If several policy options are indeed available to achieve such objective(s), states should choose the least intrusive of all equally effective means. This examination inevitably requires a comparative analysis between the measure under scrutiny and other existing policy options, which, in turn, entails not only the identification of other policy alternatives, but also the identification of their individual contribution to the pursued objective. Courts and tribunals are becoming increasingly aware of these difficulties. Thus, the WTO Appellate Body has explicitly stated:

> Certain complex public health or environmental problems may be tackled only with a comprehensive policy comprising a multiplicity of interacting measures … Substituting one element of the comprehensive policy for another would weaken the policy by reducing the synergies between the components, as well as its total effect.[11]

---

[11] Report of the Appellate Body, *Brazil – Measures Affecting Imports of Retreaded Tyres* (DS332) para 172. For further discussions on this point, and the use of evidence in necessity or proportionality tests, see T Voon, 'WTO Law and Risk Factors for Noncommunicable Diseases: A Complex Relationship', in G van Calster and D Prevost (eds), *Research Handbook on Environment, Health and the WTO* (Cheltenham: Edward Elgar, 2013), pp 390–412; A Alemanno and A Garde, 'The Emergence of EU Lifestyle Risk Regulation: New Trends in Evidence, Proportionality and Judicial Review', in H Micklitz and T Tridimas (eds), *Risk and*

5.3 Justifying measures: necessity as criterion of the general exceptions

Necessity plays an explicit role in the Article XX exceptions under the GATT, thus allowing governments to introduce measures that would otherwise violate their GATT obligations.

For example, let us consider a ban on the import of a product which poses a significant risk to human health, such as the asbestos ban introduced in France. Canada challenged the ban as a violation of, among others, Articles III and XI GATT. The EU, acting on France's behalf, rejected this claim and invoked the general exceptions of the GATT as a defence at the panel stage. Beyond the non-discrimination requirement discussed in Chapter 4, Article XX GATT also contains a 'necessity' requirement and clearly states that 'nothing in this Agreement shall be construed to prevent the adoption or enforcement by any contracting party of measures ... (b) necessary to protect human, animal or plant life or health'.

The high-profile *Brazil — Tyres* dispute is useful to understand the nuances. In this case, Brazil had introduced a ban on 'retreaded' tyres, that is, recycled tyres that have a much shorter lifespan than new tyres. The resulting increase in the number of tyre dumps had, in turn, caused health and environmental problems, as dumped tyres collect water and act as mosquito breeding grounds (among other things). Here again, much as we saw for the TBT Agreement, the Appellate Body underlined that necessity did not mean that no other options were available:

> In order to determine whether a measure is 'necessary' within the meaning of Article XX(b) of the GATT 1994, a panel must consider the relevant factors, particularly the

EU Law (Cheltenham: Edward Elgar, 2015), pp 134–168; and, more recently, M Melillo, *Weaponising Evidence: A History of Tobacco Control in International Law* (Cambridge: Cambridge University Press, 2024), particularly Chapter 3.

importance of the interests or values at stake, the extent of the contribution to the achievement of the measure's objective, and its trade restrictiveness. If this analysis yields a preliminary conclusion that the measure is necessary, this result must be confirmed by comparing the measure with possible alternatives, which may be less trade restrictive while providing an equivalent contribution to the achievement of the objective.[12]

The WTO and its organs have not provided any formal guidance or methodology to determine the important question of how the trade-restrictiveness of a measure is to be assessed. Instead, the expectation is that governments justify their position. This is why relying on a strong evidence base is crucial, as will be discussed further in section 5.4.

It is also important to note the ability of governments to mitigate concerns over their measures being more trade-restrictive than necessary, not least as a way of distinguishing the legitimate concerns of economic actors from a drive to undermine *any* regulatory activity to reduce NCDs. For example, they may allow the use of detachable labels. This may not be suitable for all products, especially if there is no clear instruction on *where* on the product the label is to be attached, but it can make a significant difference for businesses that do not then have to manufacture a different type of product for a specific export market and can instead simply produce a label that can be affixed to products before they are sold to consumers.[13]

---

[12] Appellate Body Report, *Brazil – Retreaded Tyres*, para 156.

[13] See 2018 proposals of the EU at the TBT Committee on practical compliance issues for mandatory marking and labelling requirements (G/TBT/W/534). For a critical approach to the use of stickers, see A Mitchell and P O'Brien, 'New Directions in Trade and Investment Agreements for Public Health: The Case of Alcohol Labelling', *Melbourne Journal of International Law* 21(2) (2020) 403.

5.4 The use of evidence in defending challenges to NCD prevention measures

We have seen how governments regulating to pursue legitimate public health objectives are subject to certain obligations under WTO law. However, questions persist over how governments can *demonstrate* that their measures are necessary or, where the measure has not been tried elsewhere, whether it still constitutes a legitimate restriction that can be imposed on economic actors, including the tobacco, alcohol, and food industries. There is no list of 'evidence' that can be identified at the WTO. Useful lessons on the use of evidence can nonetheless be drawn from a selection of specific disputes.

We highlight five important points here.

First, while there is flexibility in what can be relied upon, it is important to ensure that adduced evidence is rigorous. In the *Australia – Tobacco Plain Packaging* dispute, the body of literature that the Australian government submitted was subject to criticism by the complainants.[14] Individual studies where singled out and their methodological bases attacked, although they had been peer reviewed and published in respected journals. Reports were commissioned to challenge the working assumptions of the studies the government relied upon, and indeed the wider premise of their existence, including – among other lines of attack – that public health scholars who had undertaken these studies were biased in favour of positive public health outcomes.[15]

The panel in this dispute, whose report was not appealed, rejected these criticisms. Importantly, it provided an explanation of what was required as a matter of law. In particular, it explicitly stated:

---

[14] *Australia – Tobacco Plain Packaging* DS435/441/458/467.

[15] Panel Report, *Australia – Tobacco Plain Packaging* DS435/441/458/467, paras 7.525–7.538.

Overall, we do not consider that we are in a position to draw definitive conclusions on the methodological merits of each individual study referred to in relation to the impact of plain packaging on the various outcomes that they measure … Nor, indeed, do we consider that it would be appropriate for us to do so. Rather, as described above, what we must consider is the extent to which the body of evidence before us, as a whole, provides a reasonable basis in support of the proposition for which it is being invoked. In this assessment, to the extent that scientific evidence is being relied upon, we must determine whether such evidence has the 'necessary scientific and methodological rigor to be considered reputable science' according to the standards of the relevant scientific community, as well as the extent to which its use in support of the measures at issue is 'objective and coherent'.[16]

Noting that there may well be places where the literature could be more robust, the panel emphasized that the burden of proof did not require – to be discharged by Australia – that the literature as a body of evidence had to be *perfect*:

We are not persuaded that the complainants have demonstrated that this body of evidence, taken as a whole, lacks methodological rigour to such an extent that it should be considered not to constitute reputable science according to the standards of the relevant scientific community, or that Australia's reliance on it in these proceedings is not 'objective and coherent'.[17]

---

[16] Panel Report, *Australia – Tobacco Plain Packaging* DS435/441/458/467, para 7.627.
[17] Panel Report, *Australia – Tobacco Plain Packaging* DS435/441/458/467, para 7.638.

Panels will limit themselves to examining whether the evidence is sound. They will not undertake a scientific review of each of the pieces of evidence adduced by a government in support of the measures it has adopted to prevent NCDs and promote better health for all. More generally, it is important to highlight that courts and tribunals neither have the resources nor the expertise to engage in such assessments. Moreover, they are usually careful not to substitute their assessments to that of the regulating governments, particularly when the matters that these governments seek to address are urgent and complex and they have a broad margin of discretion to determine the extent to which they intend to act and the means they intend to deploy to this effect. The more governments have a wide margin of discretion, as is the case in public health, the more such an approach is indeed warranted. This is particularly important as powerful industry actors, including tobacco, alcohol, and food MNCs, tend to rely on lobbying strategies that consist in challenging both the nature and the quality of the evidence, often through relying on unscientific methodologies and/or denigrating the work of established scientists working to promote public health. They do so both directly and indirectly, through the use of front groups that speak on their behalf, notwithstanding the conflicts of interests that motivate their challenging stance.[18]

Second, measures do not need to be based on a unanimous scientific view or, indeed, majority view. In the *EC – Beef Hormones* dispute, which related to SPS measures (where the requirements to base measures on scientific evidence are stricter), the Appellate Body was at pains to note:

---

[18] See, for example, the challenge to the Nutri Score FoPNL scheme in Europe by two individuals with close ties to the food industry, discussed in A Garde et al, 'Unpacking Front-of-Pack Nutrition Labelling Research: When the Food Industry Produces "Science" as Part of Its Lobbying Strategies', *World Nutrition* 15(3) (2024) 63.

In most cases, responsible and representative governments tend to base their legislative and administrative measures on 'mainstream' scientific opinion. In other cases, equally responsible and representative governments may act in good faith on the basis of what, at a given time, may be a divergent opinion coming from qualified and respected sources.[19]

Third, there is scope for governments to experiment, provided that they do so in a logical (reasonable) manner and based on the evidence available to them. For example, in the *Brazil – Tyres* dispute, Brazil defended its ban on the import of retread tyres which are more likely to fail and be disposed of in tyre dumps, where they act as both health and environmental risks as they become a breeding ground for mosquitos and catch on fire. In its decision, the Appellate Body specifically acknowledged the reality of policy making in relation to complex societal challenges:

We recognize that certain complex public health or environmental problems may be tackled only with a comprehensive policy comprising a multiplicity of interacting measures. In the short-term, it may prove difficult to isolate the contribution to public health or environmental objectives of one specific measure from those attributable to the other measures that are part of the same comprehensive policy. Moreover, the results obtained from certain actions – for instance, measures adopted in order to attenuate global warming and the climate crisis, or certain preventive actions to reduce the incidence of diseases that may manifest themselves only after a certain period of time – can only be evaluated with the benefit of time. In order to justify an import ban under Article XX(b) [the exception relied upon by Brazil in this case], a panel must be satisfied that it brings about a material contribution to the achievement of

---

[19] Appellate Body Report, *EC – Beef Hormones* (DS26/48), para 194.

its objective. Such a demonstration can of course be made by resorting to evidence or data, pertaining to the past or the present, that establish that the import ban at issue makes a material contribution to the protection of public health or environmental objectives pursued. This is not, however, the only type of demonstration that could establish such a contribution. Thus, a panel might conclude that an import ban is necessary on the basis of a demonstration that the import ban at issue is apt to produce a material contribution to the achievement of its objective. This demonstration could consist of quantitative projections in the future, or qualitative reasoning based on a set of hypotheses that are tested and supported by sufficient evidence.[20]

Fourth, a robust evidence base is important, particularly at times when a WTO Member wishes to introduce a measure and there is no commonly agreed international standard on which it can base this measure.[21] As will be discussed in the next chapter, they will in such cases have to provide greater detail in their notifications under the TBT Agreement. Suffice it to say at this point that, to both notify and be prepared for discussion at (and around) the TBT Committee, WTO Members need to have their evidence ready as a core line of defence, and such evidence must be sufficient to provide a reasonable basis for the claims they make.

Article 2.9 of the TBT Agreement

2.9 Whenever a relevant international standard does not exist or the technical content of a proposed technical regulation is not in accordance with the technical content of relevant international standards, and if the technical regulation may have a significant effect on trade of other Members, Members shall:

---

[20] Appellate Body Report, *Brazil – Tyres* (DS332), para 151.
[21] Article 2.9 of the TBT Agreement. The role of standards is examined in greater detail in Chapter 6.

2.9.1 publish a notice in a publication at an early appropriate stage, in such a manner as to enable interested parties in other Members to become acquainted with it, that they propose to introduce a particular technical regulation;

2.9.2 notify other Members through the Secretariat of the products to be covered by the proposed technical regulation, together with a brief indication of its objective and rationale. Such notifications shall take place at an early appropriate stage, when amendments can still be introduced and comments taken into account;

2.9.3 upon request, provide to other Members particulars or copies of the proposed technical regulation and, whenever possible, identify the parts which in substance deviate from relevant international standards;

2.9.4 without discrimination, allow reasonable time for other Members to make comments in writing, discuss these comments upon request, and take these written comments and the results of these discussions into account.

Fifth, we will briefly note here that the WHO itself cannot be a party to disputes at the WTO, as it is not a WTO Member. However, it has been granted observer status in the WTO so that it can follow discussions at the WTO concerning matters of interest to the organization – for example, those at the TBT Committee which relate to tobacco, alcohol, or food packaging measures. Moreover, its views can be sought as part of dispute settlement,[22] as was done in the *Australia – Tobacco*

---

[22] Article 13(1) DSU: 'Each panel shall have the right to seek information and technical advice from any individual or body which it deems appropriate'; and Article 13(2) DSU: Panels may seek information from any relevant source and may consult experts to obtain their opinion on certain aspects of the matter. With respect to a factual issue concerning a scientific or other technical matter raised by a party to a dispute, a panel may request an advisory report in writing from an expert review group.'

Plain Packaging case,[23] where the evidence it provided proved crucial to the outcome of the dispute.[24]

5.5 Necessity under FTAs

As was also noted in the previous chapters, FTAs may place additional requirements on governments, including enhanced consultation (the regulatory cooperation chapters that we have discussed in section 3.4), which are common in both US and EU model agreements. Following the UK's withdrawal from the EU, it also includes them within its commitments as a party to 'rolled over' EU (now UK) FTAs.[25]

FTAs may also include *additional* requirements to those required under WTO rules to provide further evidence, or conduct additional steps in the regulatory process.[26] For example, much is made of the distinction between risk assessment (commonly characterized as a scientific process) and

---

[23] See https://www.who.int/westernpacific/news/item/26-09-2012-who-gives-full-support-to-australia-s-plain-tobacco-packaging. In a similar vein, both the WHO and the PAHO supported Uruguay when its tobacco packaging measures were challenged by Philip Morris before an international arbitration tribunal, as will be discussed in Chapter 8.

[24] We cannot discuss evidence in further detail in this short book; however, see M Melillo's excellent book on the topic: *Weaponising Evidence: A History of Tobacco Control in International Law* (Cambridge: Cambridge University Press, 2024), specifically Chapter 4 on strategic evidentiary challenges against tobacco control measures where she discusses the use of evidence in industry-led challenges against novel policy measures such as tobacco plain packaging.

[25] See, for example, the US-model CPTPP, the text of which is reflected in the FTAs concluded between the UK and Australia and between the UK and New Zealand, as discussed in J Larik, 'Imitation as Flattery: The UK's Trade Continuity Agreements and the EU's Normative Foreign Policy', 34(4) *EJIL* (2023) 801.

[26] In the context of SPS chapters, see M Wagner, 'The Future of SPS Governance: SPS-Plus or SPS-Minus', *JWT* 51(3) (2017) 445.

risk management (the political set of decisions, weighing and balancing the findings of risk assessment within a wider set of policy objectives).[27] Under the TBT Agreement, there is no requirement to undergo a risk assessment or risk management, though, as we have seen, good decision making and the obligations to identify the legitimate objectives that meet the policy aim in the least trade-restrictive manner possible would customarily include risk assessments. By contrast, under the SPS Agreement there *is* a specific obligation to conduct a risk assessment,[28] although there is no formal requirement to conduct a risk management per se. However, under the SPS chapter of CPTPP, there is a requirement to conduct both a risk assessment and a risk management. There is concern that this has made the requirements of the SPS Agreement 'stricter' and has reduced governments' policy space. Yet, it would be better to view this provision in the context in which it was drafted – a shot across the bows of the EU which the US and most agricultural exporters have criticized for being overly cautious in its food safety measures. Thus, the additional references to 'scientific evidence' and risk management in the US-drafted agreements are a confirmation of the requirements of the WTO SPS Agreement as they understand them.

While a process of risk assessment and risk management (as problematic as that neat distinction may be) will likely be conducted by governments, for those that have these additional commitments under FTAs, it is important to be able to *present* what they have done as risk assessment-risk management exercises. Tribunals called upon to adjudicate trade disputes are wary of being seen to encroach upon the regulatory autonomy of governments, especially on sensitive issues such as public health. As such, they will often focus on procedural rather than substantive questions: for example, 'was the risk

---

[27] See the debates in G Messenger, *The Development World Trade Organization Law* (Oxford: Oxford University Press, 2016), Chapter 4.

[28] Article 5 of the SPS Agreement.

assessment based on sufficient scientific evidence' rather than 'this is not an issue for which there is sufficient evidence that governments can regulate'.[29]

5.6 Conclusions

There is some concern that international trade and investment obligations necessarily hamper the prevention of NCDs by requiring that policies fit into the trade and investment regimes. However, the case law is clear that governments have a significant margin of discretion under international trade law to determine both the extent to which they intend to protect public health and the means they deploy to this effect. What is crucial is how they define their objectives, as this will ultimately constitute the basis for the assessment of the compatibility of these laws and policies with international trade law. The principle of necessity requires governments, first, to tailor their NCD prevention laws and policies to the objectives they pursue, and, second, to take into account the impact that such measures have on trade and other competing interests. Such considerations must be based on robust evidence intended to demonstrate that the regulating government has reflected on three core questions: whether these measures are intended to protect legitimate public interest objectives; whether they are suitable to achieve the objectives they pursue; and whether they are proportionate and do not restrict trade more than is necessary to achieve these objectives. Therefore, the principle of necessity does not have to lead to the 'weakening' of well-designed, evidence-led NCD prevention laws and policies. Governments can regulate the tobacco, alcohol, and food industries extensively on public health grounds while

---

[29] This was the case in the *EC – Hormones* (DS26) dispute, where the EU relied upon a report of the European Parliament, which in turn referenced (limited) scientific studies rather than providing evidence of its own.

complying with the principle of necessity, as the *Australia – Tobacco Plain Packaging* dispute has confirmed. Nevertheless, the lack of clarity over the *exact* application of these obligations does present significant challenges for governments, especially those that are potentially under-resourced and/or subject to significant economic coercion by significant trading partners.

The institutional framework of the trade and investment regimes provides additional 'entry points' for economic actors. This is paradigmatically the case with the TBT Committee, where Members' views of the legal obligations on responding, regulating governments are considerably stricter than panel or Appellate Body interpretation of these obligations. This highlights the importance of a strong evidence base, providing the rationale for the measure, appropriate regulatory processes, and representatives who have been briefed and prepared, not least by public health actors who understand the complexity of preventing NCDs and can convey such complexities to their trade colleagues who will ultimately be the ones defending these measures at the TBT Committee or in other relevant trade forums. The earlier that such cross-governmental dialogues can be established, with the required support from relevant experts and civil society organizations, the more likely it will be that international trade challenges can be averted or successfully defended.

SIX

The Principle of Consistency: The Role of Standards in International Trade Law

6.1 Introduction

As discussed in Chapter 3, the international trade regime encourages predictability for businesses through notification and consultation requirements. In this way, it provides businesses with more information about conditions for trade. In a similar vein, the trade regime also seeks to encourage a consistent regulatory environment for traders. It aims to promote consistency by expecting governments to regulate, as far as possible and where suitable, along similar lines. This is why standards constitute one of the most important tools to ensure consistency: they help to avoid unnecessary additional burdens for businesses that export to multiple markets. Thus, where standards are developed, they can both capture best practice as a basis for governments' regulations as well as reduce costs for businesses that can align their production processes to existing standards on, say, food or alcohol labelling.

This chapter identifies what standards are, how they become relevant through international trade law, and the benefits in using them from an NCD prevention perspective. After introducing standards and how they are developed (section 6.2), it focuses on the ways in which the TBT Agreement incentivizes governments to use standards when they regulate to encourage consistency (section 6.3), how 'relevant international standards' are identified (section 6.4), and the impact of FTAs (section 6.5).

6.2 Standards: definition and development

The TBT Agreement defines a standard as a:

> Document approved by a recognized body, that provides, for common and repeated use, rules, guidelines or characteristics for products or related processes and production methods, with which compliance is not mandatory. It may also include or deal exclusively with terminology, symbols, packaging, marking or labelling requirements as they apply to a product, process or production method.[1]

6.2.1 'A recognized body'

Standards are not mandatory by themselves; rather, their weight has traditionally come from their utility. For example, there is no international treaty or other legally binding provision specifically *requiring* the use of ISO 216 – an international standard for paper sizes including the dimensions of (near-) ubiquitous A4. However, it is useful to have a commonly agreed-upon set of dimensions for different paper sizes.

In more politically sensitive areas, international standards can also represent an evidence-based product of consensual decision making that sets out, for example, maximum residue limits of pesticides on foodstuffs. The number of standards are

---

[1]   Annex 1(2) of the TBT Agreement.

legion and broadly fall into two groups: standards developed by standardizing bodies and private standards. National standardizing bodies (for example, the British Standards Institution [BSI]) develop their own standards and work with others on a regional (for example, the European Committee for Standardization [CEN]) and international (for example, the International Organization for Standardization [ISO]) basis. However, many more standards are also developed by nongovernmental actors: some operate at a firm level, while others originate from groups of private actors, civil society, or both together. These private standards can be influential, although they are not formal 'standards' for our purposes, as they have not been approved by a recognized body.[2] Thus, if civil society, say, was to produce a useful standard for public health purposes, then the best outcome from a regulating government's perspective would be for such a standard to provide the basis for a more traditional 'public', 'recognized' standard.

For NCD prevention, one of the most important standards bodies is the Codex Alimentarius Commission (a joint FAO and WHO body) attended by representatives selected by governments.

Decision making in standardization is customarily by consensus – that is, that nobody present objects.[3] In this sense, standardization is traditionally 'bottom up' and responsive to the needs of businesses that see a benefit in developing a shared standard. Returning to the example of ISO Standard 216 setting out the dimensions for A4 paper, it benefits manufacturers of paper and printers by allowing them to trade across borders

---

[2] For example, the Green House Gas Protocols.

[3] While consensus is the dominant practice, other decision-making practices are possible. This is recognized in the Explanatory Note to Annex 1.2 of the TBT Agreement: 'Standards prepared by the international standardization community are based on consensus. This Agreement covers also documents that are not based on consensus.' This was confirmed in Report of the Appellate Body, *EC – Sardines* (DS231), paras 222–227.

without having to incur extra costs to adapt to different specifications in different markets. However, a key challenge arises when non-economic interests are at play: traditionally, it is the role of government regulation to ensure that negative externalities are reduced or reflected in product costs – for example, through the imposition of rules on chemical waste or deforestation. This 'top-down' approach is antithetical to the traditional development of standards. Furthermore, and very importantly for our purposes, to the extent that standards are consensus-based instruments, they can be criticized for being 'low ambition' or 'lowest common denominator' documents. This is all the more so as civil society has traditionally been reluctant to invest significant resources in prioritizing certain standards or putting their name to standards that they perceive as low-quality, not least due to the inherent reputational risk. This, in turn, reduces the impulse to drive the ambition of the standard upward. The problems are compounded because standards can be slow to develop, which may not respond to pressing public demands and require extensive resources.[4] Overall, it is nonetheless clear that the technicality of standard development does call for the more systematic engagement of civil society if standards are to reflect what is needed to effectively protect public health.

6.2.2 'Common and repeated use'

For the purposes of WTO law, a standard 'provides ... for common and repeated use, rules, guidelines or characteristics for products or related processes and production methods'. This criterion is important. It was discussed in the *Australia – Plain Packaging* dispute where the question arose whether

---

[4] This is most notable in the case of the climate crisis, where international standards bodies have been slow to respond to the call of the UN Secretary-General that they should all 'green' their standards to support the pursuit of net zero: see https://www.iso.org/news/ref2748.html

Australia could rely on the FCTC Guidelines as a relevant international standard to defend its tobacco plain packaging legislation. In this instance, the Panel focused not on the body that promulgated them or on their relevance per se, but rather whether elements of the FCTC constituted standards.[5] While the Guidelines were useful to parties, they were considered insufficiently precise or directive to be able to provide for their 'common and repeated use' and were not categorized as 'international standards' for the purposes of WTO law.[6] We will assess the significance of this classification for Australia and WTO Members more generally later on.

Questions have been raised about how specific or directive an instrument needs to be to constitute a standard in light of this test.[7] This presents a challenge as an instrument may lack precision as a consequence of the standards development process where consensus is the order of the day. The Panel did note that *elements* of a document could well constitute a relevant international standard, and thus indicated a preference for effect rather than form. This gives Members a wider range of possible options that might otherwise be expected.[8]

6.3 Standards under the TBT Agreement

Standards – especially international standards – can play an important role in supporting NCD prevention policies. For trade in goods, the rules of the WTO encourage their

---

[5]   Panel Report, *Australia – Tobacco Plain Packaging*, WT/DS434/R, WT/DS435/R, WT/DS441/R, WT/DS458/R, WT/DS467/R, paras 7.278ff.
[6]   Panel Report, *Australia – Tobacco Plain Packaging*, WT/DS434/R, WT/DS435/R, WT/DS441/R, WT/DS458/R, WT/DS467/R, para 7.330.
[7]   See R Tamiotti, 'Article 2 TBT' in M Wagner (ed), *Volume 4: Technical Barriers and SPS Measures* (Leiden: Brill, 2023).
[8]   Tamiotti (n7), and Panel Report, *Australia – Tobacco Plain Packaging*, WT/DS434/R, WT/DS435/R, WT/DS441/R, WT/DS458/R, WT/DS467/R, 7.331.

use through a core bargain: where a relevant international standard exists, Members are expected to use it as the basis of their new mandatory product requirements. If they do so, they are presumed to comply with certain obligations under the TBT Agreement and, in particular, they enjoy a presumption that their measure is no more trade-restrictive than necessary.

When designing and justifying measures, governments may (and in some cases must) draw on the work of international standards bodies to ensure that they comply with their WTO law obligations. In particular, the TBT Agreement requires governments to base their technical regulations[9] on relevant international standards.

The TBT Agreement

Article 2.4

Where technical regulations are required and relevant international standards exist or their completion is imminent, Members shall use them, or the relevant parts of them, as a basis for their technical regulations except when such international standards or relevant parts would be an ineffective or inappropriate means for the fulfilment of the legitimate objectives pursued, for instance because of fundamental climatic or geographical factors or fundamental technological problems.

Article 2.5

A Member preparing, adopting or applying a technical regulation which may have a significant effect on trade of other Members shall, upon the request of another Member, explain the justification for that technical regulation in terms of the provisions of paragraphs 2 to 4. Whenever a technical regulation is prepared, adopted or applied

---

[9]   Mandatory rules which set out product characteristics or their related processes and production methods. This may include terminology or definitions, or packaging or labelling requirements.

> for one of the legitimate objectives explicitly mentioned in paragraph 2, and is in accordance with relevant international standards, it shall be rebuttably presumed not to create an unnecessary obstacle to international trade.

In other words, where an international standard exists and a government has developed its technical regulation in accordance with it, the government is in a strong position to defend such regulation if it is challenged under WTO law, as Article 2(5) lays down a (rebuttable) presumption of compliance that the measure was necessary, as was discussed in Chapter 5.

Governments that intend to adopt technical regulations can follow different routes depending on whether 'relevant international standards' exist or not, and bearing in mind the importance of the TBT Agreement for NCD prevention laws and policies, particularly as they relate to product composition, labelling, and packaging. These options are demonstrated in Figure 6.1.

The first point to note is that while Members are required to use a relevant international standard (or parts thereof) as the basis of their technical regulation (note the mandatory 'shall' in Article 2.4 of the TBT Agreement quoted earlier), they are not required to do so in all instances. For example, a government may consider that an international standard is not an effective or appropriate means of fulfilling the legitimate objective(s) it pursues. A clear example of this is from the major dispute *US – Country of Origin Labelling (COOL)* on packaging, where the US successfully argued before a panel that an international standard on labelling of pre-packaged foods (CXS 1-1985) was ineffective and inappropriate to fulfil its objective. Specifically, the US wanted to ensure that customers were able to see where the animals in meat packages had been born, raised, and slaughtered, and this standard was considered inadequate to fulfil the US's objective of improving consumer information as it focused exclusively on the country where

Figure 6.1: The relationship between international standards and technical regulations

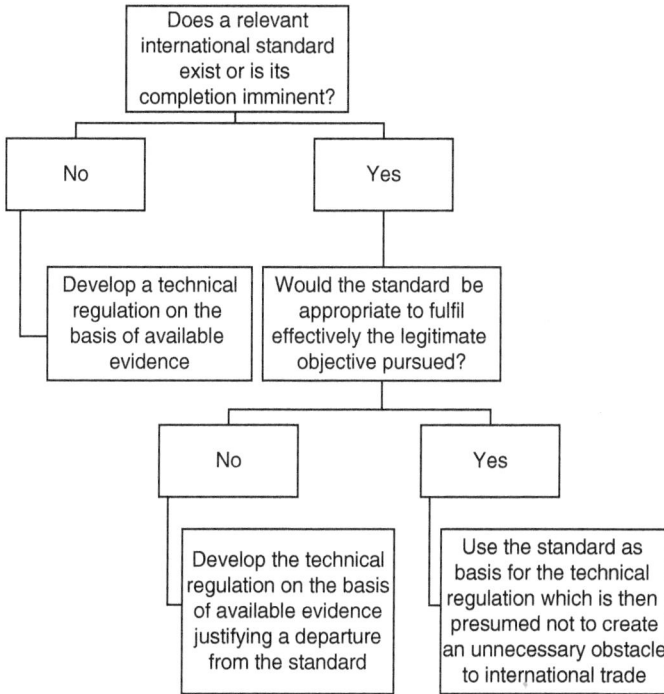

the *processing* of food took place (that is, its transformation into the final product).[10]

Nonetheless, in terms of policy design and delivery, the existence of a relevant standard that can be relied upon provides multiple benefits. First and foremost, the regulating government can enjoy a (rebuttable) presumption that its measure complies with some of the most challenging elements of the TBT Agreement, namely that there is no less trade-restrictive alternative measure reasonably available (see

---

[10] Panel Report, *US – COOL* (DS384), paras 7.732–7.735.

Chapter 5). This is particularly useful in intergovernmental discussions ahead of any formal dispute as it responds to one of the most challenging complaints – namely, that an objective could be met by another hypothetical, less trade-restrictive policy option. As was discussed previously when analysing the necessity of a measure, this complaint (based on Article 2.2 of the TBT Agreement) is commonly used and is often presented in an overly conservative manner as governments are challenged over their new public health measures. To be able to respond that the measure is indeed no more trade-restrictive than necessary therefore confers a strategic advantage.[11] Second, a measure that is based on an international standard is also subject to less onerous notification requirements (see Chapter 3).

For governments concerned about the pressure that will be placed on them at the TBT Committee, such a shield is valuable. Nonetheless, it is not always easy to either identify such a 'relevant international standard' or to use it effectively in order to benefit from the presumption under Article 2.4 of the TBT Agreement.

6.4 Relevant international standards

For a standard to be 'a relevant international standard' for the purposes of the TBT Agreement, it must both be relevant and have been produced by a recognized international body.[12]

The first limb of this test – relevance – has not proven to be a particularly contentious point in the law to date. All that is required is that the standard should 'bear upon, relate to or be pertinent to' the technical regulation in question.[13]

---

[11] There will be limits if and when governments have undertaken additional commitments under FTAs, as discussed previously.

[12] *US – Tuna II* (DS381) Report of the Appellate Body, paras 350ff.

[13] *EC – Sardines* (DS231) Panel Report, para 7.68.

More challenging is that the standard be produced by a recognized standards body. While the SPS Agreement lists three such bodies,[14] the TBT Agreement does not. Nor does it give clear guidance. It has therefore been left to the WTO Appellate Body to provide that missing guidance, which has ruled that the membership of such bodies must be open to the bodies of all WTO Members.[15] Thus, regional standard-setting bodies (such as the CEN) do not count as an international standards body for the purposes of WTO law. Similarly, documents that are otherwise useful but come from nonstandardization bodies cannot be considered relevant international standards; this is likely to be the case for the nutrient profiles published by the different regional offices of the WHO.[16]

6.4.1 Using relevant international standards

This raises another important question: *if* a relevant international standard exists, how is it to be used by a government? Standards can include significant detail, but this is not always the case, and, in any event, their nature is not the same as a regulation or piece of legislation. Instead, they may serve as definitional tools or benchmarks. For example, in the *EC – Sardines* dispute, Peru challenged the EU for its internal rules that only accepted a single species of fish as suitable for being sold as 'sardines' – unsurprisingly, a species only caught in European waters. Peru raised the fact that an existing Codex standard, which provided a longer list of species of fish which could be identified as 'sardines' when tinned, including those fished in

---

[14] Under Annex A(3) of the SPS Agreement: the Codex Alimentarius Commission, bodies under the International Plant Protection Convention, and the World Organization for Animal Health.

[15] *US – Tuna II* (DS381), Report of the Appellate Body, paras 357–359.

[16] G Messenger, 'Free Trade Agreements as Sites of Economic Diplomacy: Agreeing Common Standards for Sustainable Development', *World Trade Review* (2025) 13.

Pacific waters, had not been used by the EU as the basis for the definitional elements of its regulation.[17] As a result, the fish caught and exported by Peruvian fishers could not be sold as 'sardines' in the EU, a clear disadvantage in the European market. Both the panel and the Appellate Body in that dispute agreed that the Codex standard (STAN-94) was the 'relevant international standard' and the EU had failed to use it as the basis for its technical regulation, thus violating Article 2.4 of the TBT Agreement.

Moreover, it may well be necessary to adjust the standard in basing any national measure on it – for example, considering geographical or technological differences between governments. WTO rules themselves acknowledge that standards are unlikely to be used by governments without any adjustment; some elements may not be appropriate for the objectives they pursue, or they may otherwise need to adapt the standard to their specific national circumstances.[18]

Although the existence of an international standard is useful to base one's measure, we will sound two important notes of caution and discuss low-ambition/weak international standards (section 6.4.1.1) before turning to vague and imprecise international standards (section 6.4.1.2), using examples directly relevant to the prevention of NCDs.

6.4.1.1 Low-ambition or weak international standards

First, there is a risk that in a rush to agree an international standard, international partners will agree something that is so weak as to be worse than no standard at all if, for example, it reflects industry preferences around how the risks associated with the consumption of alcohol or unhealthy food are presented. It is arguable that in such a case, no international standard is preferable to a standard that does not reflect the

---

[17] Report of the Appellate Body, *EC – Sardines* (DS231).

[18] Article 2.4 of the TBT Agreement, second sentence.

existing evidence base. Such a substandard standard (one might name it) would be used by industry actors to claim that any technical regulation a WTO Member may adopt to protect public health is unnecessarily restrictive of trade and therefore in breach of Article 2.2 of the TBT Agreement, even if the regulation in question rests on a solid evidence base. The problem is compounded by the fact that the development of international standards in areas that raise complex and particularly sensitive issues of public interest often take years to develop and adopt, increasing the risk that such standards become somewhat outdated and less likely to serve their purposes.

The ongoing discussions at the Codex Alimentarius Commission on alcohol labelling vividly illustrate these difficulties.

6.4.1.1.1 Codex standards and alcohol labelling[19]

Discussions on alcohol labelling are ongoing at the Codex Alimentarius Commission. However, they do not align (at least to date) with the requirements of the WHO Global Alcohol Action Plan 2022–2030 or the WHO Global Action Plan on the Prevention and Control of NCDs, which call on governments around the world to effectively address alcohol-related harm, and specifically provide consumers with clear and appropriate information (including health warnings) about the content of alcoholic beverages and the harms associated with alcohol consumption. The WHO Global Alcohol Action Plan also entrusts the WHO Secretariat to 'develop international guidance on labelling of alcoholic beverages to inform consumers about the content of products and health risks associated with their consumption' and to support the 'development and implementation of warning labels'.

---

[19] We thank Dr Nikhil Gokani at the University of Essex for his insights on this process and the information he has provided on this case study.

6.4.1.1.1.1 Existing standards on food labelling that are relevant to alcohol-harm prevention

The Codex General Standard for the Labelling of Prepackaged Foods CXS 1-1985 (2018 revision) is relevant to alcohol labelling, as the definition of food is broad and includes alcoholic beverages. It states that an ingredients list should be mandatory. It also specifies that other information may be displayed on the label, provided that: (1) it does not conflict with mandated information; and (2) it complies with the general principle that information cannot be false, misleading, deceptive, or likely to create an erroneous impression regarding its character.

The Guidelines on Nutrition Labelling CAC/GL 2-1985 (last revised in 2021) provide that a nutrient declaration should be mandatory for all pre-packaged foods for which nutrition or health claims are made as well as for all other pre-packaged foods, except where national circumstances would not support such declarations.

The Codex Commission has also developed General Guidelines on Claims CAC/GL 1-197, which determine which claims should be prohibited, and the conditions that claims should meet. In particular, if claims cannot be substantiated, they should be prohibited.

The Guidelines for Use of Nutrition and Health Claims CAC/GL 23-1997 cover nutrition claims (for example, 'this beverage contains low alcohol') and health claims (for example, 'moderate alcohol consumption raises your levels of good cholesterol'). In particular, these Guidelines call for restrictions on alcohol nutrition claims: 'The only nutrition claims permitted shall be those relating to energy, protein, carbohydrate, and fat and components thereof, fibre, sodium and vitamins and minerals for which Nutrient Reference Values have been laid down in the Codex Guidelines for Nutrition Labelling.'

The General Guidelines on Claims also support the ban of alcohol health claims, calling on Members to:

have a clear regulatory framework for qualifying and/ or disqualifying conditions for eligibility to use the specific claim, including the ability of competent national authorities to prohibit claims made for foods that contain nutrients or constituents in amounts that increase the risk of disease or an adverse health-related condition. The health claim should not be made if it encourages or condones excessive consumption of any food or disparages good dietary practice.

6.4.1.1.1.2 Towards a specific standard on alcohol health warning labels? Ongoing discussions

One could argue that, to date, there is no 'relevant' international standard on alcohol health warnings, as Codex standards do not currently cover such warnings explicitly. Nevertheless, as the list of mandatory information has been listed in the Codex General Standard for the Labelling of Prepackaged Foods, it is more likely that 'relevant' international standards do exist. Therefore, the question for WTO Members challenged at the TBT Committee is to determine how far they can depart from the 'relevant' international standard and adopt more restrictive regulations to warn consumers of the health risks associated with alcohol consumption. To this end, they will need to demonstrate: (1) that the international standards listed earlier are an ineffective or inappropriate means for the fulfilment of the legitimate objectives they pursue; and (2) that the rules they adopt do not create unnecessary obstacles to international trade and are well suited to fulfil these objectives (as discussed in Chapter 5).

Alcohol health warnings have given rise to vivid discussions at the TBT Committee.[20] Following the pressure exerted

---

[20] Data from 'Navigating Trade Challenge at the World Trade Organization to Prevent Non-Communicable Diseases and Promote Better Health for All' (NIHR204663).

on them, some governments have had to review their plans to implement warning labels on alcoholic beverages,[21] whereas in recent years, others have managed to overcome the challenges encountered, notably with the support of the public health community and academics working at the trade/health interface.[22]

The adoption of an effective evidence-based international standard on alcohol warning labelling would support these efforts and facilitate the work that some WTO Members do to prevent NCDs, thus promoting a high level of public health protection.

Discussions on alcohol health warnings have been ongoing at Codex since the WHO raised the issue in 2017.[23] In particular, the Committee on Food Labelling noted in 2021 that 'there was common ground on which to proceed with the work'.[24] It was agreed that Russia, the EU, and India, with assistance from the WHO and the European Alcohol Policy Alliance (Eurocare), would prepare a discussion paper for consideration at the next meeting of the Committee. However, no discussion paper was submitted. Therefore, the WHO[25] and Eurocare[26] each submitted their own discussion papers to keep the matter on the Codex agenda. The Codex Alimentarius Commission

---

[21] P Barlow, D Gleeson, P O'Brien, and R Labonte, 'Industry influence over global alcohol policies via the World Trade Organization: a qualitative analysis of discussions on alcohol health warning labelling, 2010–19', *Lancet Global Health* 10 (2022) e429–37.

[22] In particular, Ireland, which has developed comprehensive and mandatory alcohol warning labels.

[23] CCEXEC73 (2017), CAC40 (2017) and CCFL44 (October 2017).

[24] Report of the Forty-Sixth Session of the Codex Committee on Food Labelling (REP21/FL) 8–18 2021.

[25] Codex Alimentarius Commission, Comments of WHO (FL/47 CRD18), 15–19 May 2023.

[26] Codex Alimentarius Commission, Comments of Eurocare (FL/47 CRD19), 15–19 May 2023.

opened a consultation,[27] and the matter was discussed again at the meeting of the Committee on Food Labelling that took place from 27 October to 1 November 2024. No standard has yet been adopted, notwithstanding the adoption of the WHO Global Action Plan in May 2022 and its explicit call on the international community to develop and implement alcohol health warning labels.

6.4.1.2 Imprecise or vague international standards

Second, a standard may be insufficiently precise to serve its purpose of creating consistency across regulation, as the discussions at the Codex Alimentarius Commission on FoPNL exemplify.

6.4.1.2.1 International trade and the regulation of front-of-pack nutrition labelling in Latin America

As just noted in relation to alcohol health warnings, Codex has long provided guidance on food labelling and the regulation of nutrition and health claims to promote better understanding of the nutritional quality of the food that consumers purchase. However, it is only recently that the Codex Alimentarius Commission has discussed the supplementation of back-of-pack nutrition labelling with 'at a glance' FoPNL.

FoPNL informs consumers about the nutritional quality of food, and improves both the information environment in which they make food choices and the nutritional quality of their individual food choices. It also incentivizes manufacturers to improve the nutritional quality of the food they produce through reformulation.

---

[27] Circular letter asking state members and observers to comment on how work on developing alcohol standards should proceed ahead of the next Codex meeting in Ottawa from 27 October to 1 November 2024.

The Latin American region has pioneered legal developments in this area.[28] Many governments in the region have mandated FoPNL schemes, alongside other measures intended to prevent diet-related diseases, and improve public health. Two distinct FoPNL schemes have emerged in the region:

- warning labels, which alert consumers to the content of higher quantities of specific nutrients of concern. First implemented in Chile in 2016, they have also been adopted in Peru, Uruguay, Mexico, Argentina, Colombia, Venezuela, and Brazil, with variations from one country to the other; and
- multiple 'traffic light' labels, which are nutrient-specific graded schemes. First introduced in the UK in 2013, this has since been implemented in Bolivia and Ecuador in Latin America.

Although FoPNL schemes are all designed to increase consumer understanding and help consumers make healthier food choices, different FoPNL schemes follow different specific objectives. Warning labels have been introduced to deter consumers from purchasing processed products high in nutrients of concern, while multiple traffic light labels aim to both discourage less healthy choices and promote healthier ones. In sharp contrast to what has been done in many countries around the world where FoPNL schemes remain voluntary,[29] FoPNL schemes have been introduced on a mandatory basis, following Chile's lead, in all the Latin American countries listed earlier. This explains why these countries have faced so many challenges at the TBT Committee.

---

[28] FAO, PAHO and UNICEF, *Front-of-pack nutrition labelling in Latin America and the Caribbean – Guidance note* (2023).

[29] N Gokani, 'Front-of-pack Nutrition Labelling: A *Tussle* between EU Food Law and National Measures', *European Law Review* 47(2) (2022) 153.

Three closely related arguments have been recurring at the TBT Committee: (1) the failure of relevant WTO Members to comply with existing standards; (2) the lack of evidence underpinning the proposed measures by these WTO Members; and (3) the unnecessarily trade-restrictive nature of these measures – all pointing to the violation of Article 2.2 of the TBT Agreement. Ultimately, these arguments have successfully been rebutted, and the measures have now been implemented. One should also note that opposition to schemes more recently introduced has also notably lessened in comparison with the opposition that Chile and other 'early adopters' of FoPNL schemes in the region faced.[30]

It is now clear that WTO Members can (and should) develop and implement evidence-based FoPNL schemes. However, and as emphasized throughout this book, gaining such certainty has come at a cost for all governments implicated in the defence of their schemes. This cost has stemmed, in large part, from the major discrepancy noted throughout this book between the interpretation of the TBT Agreement by WTO organs such as the Appellate Body, one the one hand, and its instrumental, self-serving interpretation by industry actors, on the other hand.[31] Such a discrepancy arguably reinforces the need for the international community to adopt a common position supporting the development and implementation of evidence-based FoPNL schemes which can serve both international trade and public health imperatives.

In May 2016, the Codex Committee on Food Labelling, after considering proposals from the International Association

---

[30] Data from 'Navigating Trade Challenge at the World Trade Organization to Prevent Non-Communicable Diseases and Promote Better Health for All' (NIHR204663).

[31] For an excellent analysis of this discrepancy in the Chilean context, see T Dorlach and P Mertenskötter, 'Interpreters of International Economic Law: Corporations and Bureaucrats in Contest over Chile's Nutrition Label', *Law & Society Review* 54(3) (2020) 571.

of Consumer Food Organizations, and the governments of New Zealand and Costa Rica, agreed to establish a Working Group in order to explore the possibility of revising the Codex nutrition labelling standards.[32] In 2021, the Codex Guidelines on food labelling were revised. They now include Annex 2. It is intended to 'provide general guidance to assist in the development of [FoPNL]' on pre-packaged food.

The Guidelines list the following principles:

- Only one FoPNL system should be recommended by government in each country. However, if multiple FoPNL systems coexist, these should be complementary rather than contradictory to each other.
- FoPNL should be applied to the food in a manner consistent with the corresponding nutrient declaration for that food.
- FoPNL should align with evidence-based national or regional dietary guidance or, in its absence, health and nutrition policies. Consideration should be given to the nutrients and/or the food groups which are discouraged and/or encouraged by these documents.
- FoPNL should present information in a way that is easy to understand and use by consumers in the country or region of implementation. The format of the FoPNL should be supported by scientifically valid consumer research.
- FoNPL should be clearly visible on the package/packaging at the point of purchase under normal conditions.
- FoPNL should help consumers to make appropriate comparisons between foods.
- FoPNL should be government-led, but developed in consultation with all interested parties, including the private sector, consumers, academia, and public health associations.

---

[32] Available at https://www.fao.org/fao-who-codexalimentarius/ sh-proxy/en/?lnk=1&url=https%253A%252F%252Fworkspace.fao. org%252Fsites%252Fcodex%252FMeetings%252FCX-714-43%252 FReport%252FREP16_FLe.pdf

- FoPNL should be implemented in a way that facilitates the broad availability of FoPNL for consumer use.
- FoPNL should be accompanied by a consumer education/ information programme to increase consumer understanding and use of FoPNL in line with government recommendations.
- FoPNL should be monitored and evaluated to determine effectiveness and impact.

Importantly, these Guidelines recognize the need for government-led FoPNL schemes. However, they stop short of calling for mandatory schemes. Moreover, while they support 'evidence-based', 'clearly visible', 'easy to understand' schemes, they do not specifically call on governments to adopt interpretive FoPNL schemes.

This is unsurprising, considering: (1) that discussions at the Codex Alimentarius Commission have become more political as membership has grown from 44 Members in 1962 to 189 Members (188 member countries and the EU as a member organization); and (2) more specifically, that the discussions on FoPNL have been characterized by significantly higher representation of food industry compared to public health actors.[33]

That said, the revision of the Food Labelling Guidelines is welcome. These Guidelines will support the implementation by governments around the world of effective FoPNL schemes. This, in turn, will allow them to meet their commitments under both the TBT Agreement and the WHO Global Action Plan on the Prevention and Control of NCDs, which, in its revised version, specifically lists the adoption of FoPNL as one of the 'best buy' policies WHO recommends.[34]

---

[33] A Thow, A Jones, C Huckel Schneider and R Labonte, 'Increasing the Public Health Voice in Global Decision-Making on Nutrition Labelling', *Globalization and Health* 16(1) (2020) 3.

[34] WHO, *Tackling NCDs: Best Buys and Other Recommended Interventions for the Prevention and Control of Noncommunicable Diseases* (Geneva: WHO, 2nd edn, 2024).

Thirdly, and finally, it is important to note that even in the absence of any international standard, regulating governments are still able to act to prevent NCDs, including through the regulation of the tobacco, alcohol, or food industries. Where new measures are based on sound available evidence, tailored to meet a specific objective, and the effects of the measure have been reflected upon and, where appropriate, adequately mitigated, then these interventions are likely to be on a strong footing, as was discussed in Chapter 5.

6.5 Consistency under FTAs

The use of standards also arises as an element of FTAs, albeit to a lesser extent for NCDs and public health. Some general commitments can have an effect: for example, the US-Mexico-Canada FTA requires the parties to provide an *explicit* justification for not using a relevant international standard where appropriate, and the evidence on which their decision is based.[35]

Although FTAs could create additional obligations that could further restrict what governments can do when tackling NCDs, this is one area where it may be possible to take advantage of FTAs to the advantage of public health. It is now common for FTAs to include annexes that cover sectoral issues, such as cosmetics and pharmaceuticals.[36] Some will provide additional requirements identifying specific standards bodies or standards as 'relevant' for the parties to the agreement. An example would be the EU and UK FTAs as they relate to motor vehicles and specific standard body historically preferred by the EU.[37] Currently, the public health dimensions of these sectoral

---

[35] Article 11.5.6 USMCA.

[36] For example, the UK–Australia FTA.

[37] United Nations Economic Commission for Europe (UNECE), World Forum for the harmonization of vehicle regulations (WP.29).

annexes are limited, but with increasing attention placed on labelling requirements for food and alcoholic beverages, one could envisage – as we have noted earlier in the TBT context – that governments explicitly acknowledge certain instruments as the relevant standards as between them, even if there is trepidation elsewhere.[38]

6.6 Conclusions

International standards play an important role in trade, both reducing costs for traders and enhancing consistency across different national regulatory approaches. This importance is reflected in the international trade regime, which encourages their use and provides specific benefits for those that base their mandatory technical regulations on relevant international standards. At the same time, in the absence of sufficiently specific, evidence-based relevant international standards, governments retain their ability to introduce measures, particularly to protect health and prevent NCDs. The international trade regime here again demonstrates an ability to address potentially competing priorities and interests in a balanced manner. Relevant international standards are best used as practical tools rather than envisaged as a straitjacket preventing governments from regulating the tobacco, alcohol, and food industries effectively to prevent NCDs and promote better health.

Nevertheless, the strategic importance of international standards is such, particularly when governments are called upon to defend their public health measures at the TBT or other committee, that the public health community need to rally round governments and increase their presence in

---

[38] For models on how this might happen, see G Messenger, 'Free Trade Agreements as Sites of Economic Diplomacy: Agreeing Common Standards for Sustainable Development' *World Trade Review* (2025).

forums where standards relevant to the prevention of NCDs are discussed, adopted, and revised in order to ensure that the arguments that industry actors put forward again and again in these forums are not left unchallenged and that the standards do reflect existing evidence.

SEVEN

The Protection of Intellectual Property and the Trade Regime

7.1 Introduction

IP rights are granted to persons over the creation of their minds. They usually give the creator an exclusive right over the use of their creations for a certain period of time. The IP system is seen as a tool of public policy intended to promote economic, social, and cultural welfare by stimulating creative work and technological innovation, and by enabling their benefits to reach the public. In the absence of IP protection, it is difficult for creators to extract economic value or 'appropriate' financial returns from their work, or indeed to influence how they are used. Thus, IP diminishes the risk of underinvestment in socially beneficial creative and innovative work.

IP rights have been at the core of several challenges against labelling or marketing rules adopted by states as part of their NCD prevention efforts. In particular, questions have arisen concerning the compatibility of labelling and marketing restrictions with the WTO TRIPS Agreement which protect trademarks and constitutes the focus of this chapter, as well as with international investment agreements which protect foreign investors from expropriation and are discussed in the following chapter.[1]

TRIPS is part of the WTO Agreement (Annex 1C) and is binding on each WTO Member. It is the most comprehensive multilateral agreement on IP and aims to protect IP rights, while ensuring that measures and procedures to enforce IP rights do not themselves become barriers to legitimate trade.[2] Although it is important to note that IP protection is enacted and enforced at a national level, in each jurisdiction, TRIPS specifically requires that all WTO Members provide a certain level of IP protection within their own legal systems.

The TRIPS Council, also consisting of all Members, is one of the three sectoral councils operating under the General Council.[3] It is the body responsible for administering TRIPS and monitoring its operation, promoting transparency.[4] The Council meets in Geneva formally three to four times a year, and informally where necessary.

TRIPS sets out the minimum standards of protection that Members must provide, allowing them to exceed these standards if they so wish. Importantly for our purposes, TRIPS recognizes the right of governments to adopt measures for public health and other public interest reasons, and to prevent

---

[1] Challenges invoking the fundamental right to property, which has been interpreted to include IP, have also been mounted against measures adopted to prevent NCDs on the basis of national or regional constitutional and human rights law. However, they are not discussed in this book as they are not within the scope of international trade and investment law.

[2] These overarching objectives should be read in light of Article 7, according to which the protection and enforcement of IP rights should contribute to the promotion of technological innovation and to the transfer and dissemination of technology, to the mutual advantage of producers and users of technological knowledge and in a manner conducive to social and economic welfare, and to a balance of rights and obligations.

[3] See Chapter 2, section 2.2.

[4] See Chapter 3 on the principle of transparency.

the abuse of IP rights, provided that they are otherwise TRIPS-compliant.

TRIPS covers many areas of IP, including trademarks which are signs intended to distinguish the goods or services of one enterprise from another. After laying down general provisions and basic principles applicable to all IP rights (Articles 1–7),[5] TRIPS identifies the standards concerning the availability (section 7.3), scope (section 7.4) and use of specific rights (section 7.5), including trademarks (Articles 15–21). Before we review these three components as they relate to the prevention of NCDs, we briefly introduce the function of a trademark and why it is protected under TRIPS (section 7.2), focusing specifically on the relationship between trademark and public health protection.[6]

7.2 The function of trademarks and the rationale for their protection

Trademarks constitute a specific category of IP. They consist in a sign, or a combination of signs, capable of distinguishing the goods or services of one business from another – for example, the golden arches of the letter M for McDonald's on a red background. Trademark law prohibits third parties from using identical or similar signs in a way that would result in a likelihood of confusion. As protected distinctive signs, trademarks therefore help to ensure fair competition among producers by encouraging companies to invest in their reputation through the provision of quality products and services by protecting their goodwill. Trademarks help recoup such investment as others cannot 'free ride' by using identical or similar marks without having invested themselves.

---

[5] Articles 1–8.

[6] As this book focuses on the prevention of NCDs, we do not discuss the extensive literature on access to medicines on the control (as opposed to the prevention) of NCDs.

Trademark law also supports franchising which can result in the rapid spread of the mark all over the world.[7]

Trademarks enable consumers to distinguish between various goods and services, thus reducing the risk of confusion and helping them to assess quality, which, in turn, can save them a vast amount of 'search' and 'experience' costs. Their protection thus helps to correct information asymmetries – that is, the imbalance between buyers and sellers in the information that they possess on the quality or other characteristics of particular branded goods or services on the market.[8]

Trademarks empower their owners to shape how they present their goods, services, and brands, thus influencing the perception of consumers. While the main function of a trademark is the 'original function' which helps to distinguish branded goods and services from those of their competitors, trademarks also have a function of promoting the consumption of the goods and services they offer ('advertising function'). As such, trademarks are a means of increasing the overall size of the market by inviting consumers to buy branded goods and services. In other words, trademarks also perform an advertising function, which, in turn, raises the question of their implications in the growing prevalence of NCDs worldwide.[9]

Reflecting their role as tools of public policy, IP rights are not absolute and unlimited, but are subject to limitations and exceptions that aim to balance the legitimate interests of IP rights holders (industry) and users (consumers) so that the system as a whole can effectively meet its stated objectives.

---

[7]   The reference to 'coca-colonization' springs to mind here.

[8]   WTO, 'The Economics of TRIPS: A series of primers on economic questions concerning Trade Related Aspects of Intellectual Property Rights': https://www.wto.org/english/tratop_e/trips_e/trips_econprimer1_e.pdf

[9]   For a discussion of the expanding functions of trademarks, see in particular Case C-324/09 *L'Oréal S, et al. v. eBay International*, ECLI:EU:C:2011:474.

Table 7.1: NCD intervention and implications in IP

Intervention	Examples	IP implications
Mandatory disclosure to reflect association of consumption with health risks	Warning labels on tobacco or alcohol, front-of-pack nutrition labels	Reduced benefit from use of trademark on packaging
Restrictions on the use of voluntary commercial information/ marketing provided to promote consumption	Regulation of nutrition and health claims (for example, prohibition of health claims on alcoholic beverages; regulation of 'low in xx' on food or alcohol; prohibition of 'light' or 'mild' cigarettes); a ban on the use of brand characters and other marketing techniques (for example, use of celebrities or cartoon characters)	Reduced benefit from trademark due to limitations on use (for example, a ban on advertising to children), or potential prohibition of use of trademark in public spaces

Table 7.1 outlines how NCD interventions can have a direct implication for IP rights holders.

7.3 The availability of trademark protection: distinctiveness and registration

Any sign, or any combination of signs, capable of distinguishing the goods and services of one business from those of another must be eligible for registration as a trademark, provided that it is visually perceptible.[10] The nature of the goods or services to which a trademark is applied does not form an obstacle to

---

[10] Article 15.1 TRIPS.

registration.[11] In other words, governments cannot merely rely on the harmfulness of a given product, such as tobacco, alcohol, or unhealthy food, to refuse registration. However, they may restrict their use, as will be discussed later on. In other words, the assessment of the impact of specific goods, services, and brands on health comes at a later stage in the analysis of whether a measure complies with TRIPS.

When deciding whether a trademark can be registered, the emphasis is on distinctiveness. Signs are considered distinctive for a certain class or classes of product (for example, fizzy drinks) where consumers associate these signs with goods or services from a particular company (for example, Coca-Cola), rather than a type of product (for example, low in sugar or sugar-free). In other words, if marks are descriptive, they may not be capable of distinguishing the goods or services of one company from another unless they have subsequently acquired distinctiveness.

Where signs are not inherently capable of distinguishing the relevant goods and services, WTO Members may nonetheless allow trademark registration based on distinctiveness acquired through use.[12] The coloured sole of a shoe is one such example – something that is not inherently distinctive as a trademark, but in the case of Christian Louboutin shoes, the red sole (the 'Red Sole Mark') has been registered in multiple jurisdictions.[13]

WTO Members are also free to determine whether to allow the registration of signs that are not visually perceptible, such as sounds, smells, and tastes.

---

[11] Article 15.4 TRIPS, as interpreted in the Panel Report, *Australia – Tobacco Plain Packaging*, para 7.1847.

[12] Article 15.1 TRIPS does not oblige Members to register signs as trademarks if they are not inherently distinctive and have yet to acquire distinctiveness through use: *Australia – Tobacco Plain Packaging*.

[13] C Aranda, 'The Worldwide Trademark Battle over the Iconic Red Bottom Shoe', *Chicago-Kent Journal of Intellectual Property* (23 January 2023).

If a trademark become generic, in the sense that the mark becomes descriptive or is commonly considered as referring to an entire class of goods and no longer serves to identify their origin, it falls into the public domain (for example, mayonnaise). Many trademark laws around the world allow for registration to be cancelled when a mark has ceased to be distinctive – that is, when trademarks become generic.[14]

Under the TRIPS, initial registration and each renewal of registration of a trademark shall be for a term of no less than seven years.[15] Trademarks, like other IP rights, are territorial and valid in the jurisdiction(s) where they have been registered or otherwise acquired.

As mentioned earlier, TRIPS sets out general provisions and basic principles, including the principle of non-discrimination (both national treatment and MFN), the scope of which is broadly construed and prohibits IP protection from being granted only to nationals of a given country.[16] 'Protection' includes matters affecting the availability, acquisition, scope, maintenance, and enforcement of IP rights.

7.4 The scope of protection: a negative right to protection from unauthorized use, not a positive right to use

Under Article 16 TRIPS, owners of a registered trademark have the exclusive right to prevent unauthorised third parties from using, in the course of trade, identical or similar signs if this may create a likelihood of confusion. Such likelihood of confusion must be presumed when an identical or a similar sign is used for identical or similar goods or services.[17]

---

[14] The TRIPS Agreement provides that service marks should be protected in the same way as trademarks for goods.

[15] Article 18 TRIPS. The registration of a trademark is indefinitely renewable.

[16] See Panel Report, *Australia – Tobacco Plain Packaging*, paras 7.1771 and 7.1772.

[17] Article 16.1 TRIPS.

A registered trademark owner can exercise its right against unauthorised third parties – that is, 'all third parties not having the owner's consent'.

However, and most importantly for our purposes, TRIPS does *not* grant a positive right on trademark owners to use their registered trademark; it *only* grants the exclusive right to prevent unauthorized parties from use.[18]

The concepts of registration and use of trademarks are distinct. The use of trademarks is covered by Article 20 TRIPS (which will be discussed later on), not by Article 16.[19] Article 20 TRIPS requires that 'the use of a trademark in the course of trade shall not be *unjustifiably* encumbered by special requirements, such as use with another trademark, use in a special form or use in a manner detrimental to its capability to distinguish the goods or services of one undertaking from those of other undertakings' (emphasis added).

Measures which promote product standardization – for example, by regulating labelling or marketing practices – cannot be challenged using Article 16 TRIPS, which deals with the relationship between trademark owners and their competitors. They can only be challenged on the basis of Article 20 TRIPS, which deals with an entirely different relationship: that between trademark owners and governments acting as regulators.[20] The

---

[18] Appellate Body, *Australia – Tobacco Plain Packaging*, at paras 6.581 and 6.582.

[19] E Bonadio, 'On the nature of trademark rights: does trademark registration confer positive or negative rights?', in A Alemanno and E Bonadio (eds), *The New Intellectual Property of Health: Beyond Tobacco Plain Packaging* (Cheltenham: Edward Elgar, 2016), at page 58. On the notion of 'legitimate interests', see European Communities, Protection of Trademarks and Geographical Indications for Agricultural Products and Foodstuffs – Complaint by the United States – Report of the Panel, 15 March 2005, WT / DS174 / R, at para 7.662.

[20] M Davison and P Emerton, 'Rights, Privileges, Legitimate Interests and Justifiability: Article 20 of TRIPS and Plain Packaging of Tobacco', *American University International Law Review* 29 (2014) 505.

next section focuses on the extent to which governments can restrict the enjoyment of a trademark by its owner.

7.5 Restricting the use of a trademark: justifiable encumbrances

For the first time in *Australia – Tobacco Plain Packaging*, a WTO panel and the Appellate Body elaborated on the applicable standard of justification for encumbrances on the use of trademarks to promote public interest objectives, and the protection of public health more specifically. The Panel held that the Doha Declaration served to underscore that the term 'unjustifiably', as used in Article 20, provided Members with 'a wide degree of latitude to implement measures to protect public health'.[21]

The core obligation enshrined in Article 20 requires that three elements be established for a measure to infringe this provision:

- the existence of 'special requirements';
- that such special requirements 'encumber' the use of a trademark in the course of trade; and
- that they do so 'unjustifiably'.

A *special requirement* refers to a condition that must be complied with; has a close connection with, or specifically addresses, the 'use of a trademark in the course of trade'; and is limited in application. This includes a broad range of standardization requirements which reduce the ability of manufacturers to design the presentation of their products[22] and use their trademarks freely. The design of tobacco packaging has

---

[21] Panel Report, *Australia – Tobacco Plain Packaging*, para 7.2348.
[22] Standardization requirements are also referred to as 'space appropriation measures'.

been particularly contested, as it has become one of the last opportunities left to tobacco MNCs to promote their products and brands to consumers: from the imposition of textual warnings, the prohibition on misleading claims, and specific restrictions on health claims (for example, 'light' or 'mild' cigarettes), the imposition of combined textual and graphic warnings, enlarged warnings, to the adoption of plain packaging which prevents the use of nonword trademarks on retail packaging, while allowing the use of word trademarks only in a prescribed form. We can expect similar challenges as the food and alcohol industries become more regulated.

While traditional trademark protection used to enable and facilitate consumer choice, now it must coexist with competing policy objectives, including providing guidance on the adverse health effects stemming from the consumption of tobacco, alcohol, and unhealthy food. This is where the harmfulness of products becomes relevant to the assessment. Under TRIPS, public authorities can 'encumber a trademark' and adopt measures aimed at discouraging the consumption of such products by curbing the deceptive and promotional elements of their brands, provided that the requirements thus imposed are not unjustifiable encumbrances.

Therefore, whether a trademark is 'unjustifiably encumbered' is the crux of the matter. It is only if a given encumbrance 'lacks a justification or reason that is sufficient to support the resulting encumbrance'[23] that it infringes Article 20 TRIPS.

The following factors need to be considered in the assessment:

- the nature and extent of the encumbrance resulting from the special requirements, bearing in mind the legitimate interest of the trademark owner in using its trademark in the course of trade;

---

[23] Appellate Body Report, *Australia – Tobacco Plain Packaging*, para 6.624, referring to paras 7.2395 and 7.2396 of the Panel Report.

- the reasons for which the special requirements are applied, including any societal interests they are intended to safeguard; and
- whether these reasons provide sufficient support for the resulting encumbrance.[24]

The preamble to and Articles 7 and 8 TRIPS express a range of general objectives and principles of the TRIPS, which are relevant when examining Article 20, as the Appellate Body has recognized.[25] Article 7 reflects the search for a balanced approach to IP protection in the societal interest, taking into account the interests of both producers and users, with the overall aim of promoting social and economic welfare. Similarly, Article 8 recognizes the rights of WTO Members to adopt measures on public health and other legitimate grounds and prevent the abuse of IP rights, provided that such measures are consistent with the provision of TRIPS.

The 2001 Doha Declaration on the TRIPS Agreement and Public Health reinforces the view that Members have extensive powers to regulate and protect public health, even if this may lead to the limitations of IP rights. First, paragraph 1 of the Declaration, which defines its scope, provides that Members recognize the gravity of the public health problems affecting many developing countries, especially those resulting from HIV/AIDS, tuberculosis, malaria, and other epidemics – this (heavily negotiated) language makes it clear that the Doha Declaration is not limited to the diseases it explicitly mentions, but is broader in its application and covers NCDs. Second, paragraph 4 of the Declaration highlights that TRIPS does not, and should not, prevent Members from taking measures

---

[24] Appellate Body Report, *Australia – Tobacco Plain Packaging*, para 6.628, upholding the Panel at para 7.2430.

[25] See Panel Reports, *Australia – Tobacco Plain Packaging* and *Canada – Pharmaceuticals Patents*.

to protect public health and reaffirms their right to fully use the flexibilities available in TRIPS for this purpose. This indicates that all Members accept that they should refrain from preventing other Members from using TRIPS flexibilities.[26]

The *burden of proof* lies on the party asserting a fact; this party is therefore responsible for establishing that what it claims is true.[27] Thus, in *Australia – Tobacco Plain Packaging*, it was for the complainants (those challenging Australia's public health measures) to demonstrate that the measures amounted to special requirements and that the use of a trademark in the course of trade was unjustifiably encumbered by these requirements. As far as the *level of proof* is concerned, 'if the party bearing the burden of proof adduces evidence sufficient to raise a presumption that what is claimed is true, the burden then shifts to the other party, who will fail unless it adduces sufficient evidence to rebut the presumption'.[28] Therefore, it is for the party making the claim (in this case, challenging an NCD intervention) to put forward sufficient evidence to make a prima facie case that what is claimed is true – that is, one which, in the absence of effective refutation by the defending party, requires a panel, as a matter of law, to rule in favour of the complaining party presenting the case. Once that prima facie case is made, the onus shifts to the other party, which will fail unless it submits sufficient evidence to disprove the claim, thus rebutting the presumption. The panel's task will be to consider all evidence on record and decide whether the complainant,

---

[26] 'We agree that the TRIPS Agreement does not and should not prevent Members from taking measures to protect public health. Accordingly, while reiterating our commitment to the TRIPS Agreement, we affirm that the Agreement can and should be interpreted and implemented in a manner supportive of WTO Members' rights to protect public health, and in particular, to promote access to medicines for all' (para 4).

[27] Appellate Body Report in *Australia – Tobacco Plain Packaging*, at para 7.2158.

[28] Appellate Body Report in *US – Wool Shirts and Blouses*, at para 14.

as the party bearing the burden of proof, has convinced it of the validity of its claims to the point of establishing a prima facie case, and whether the respondent has sufficiently rebutted such a prima facie case.[29]

Importantly, the Appellate Body highlighted that the prima facie case needed to be based on evidence and legal argument put forward by the complaining party for each of the elements of the case. This means that a complaining party may not simply submit evidence and expect the panel to divine from it a claim of WTO inconsistency. Nor may a complaining party simply allege facts without relating them to its legal arguments.

WTO Members enjoy even more regulatory autonomy when encumbering the use of trademarks by special requirements, insofar as Article 20 TRIPS does not require an analysis of alternative measures.[30] Indeed, the word used in Article 20 is 'unjustifiably', not 'necessary' as in Article 8 TRIPS or in other WTO agreements, not least Article 2.2 of the TBT Agreement and Article XX GATT 1994.[31]

7.6 Extending protections in FTAs

As we have seen in previous chapters, FTAs often include an additional layer of commitments that go beyond what governments have committed to at the WTO, including

---

[29] Appellate Body Reports in *EC – Hormones*, at para 104; and *Australia – Tobacco Plain Packaging*, at para 7.2159.

[30] Appellate Body Report in *Australia – Tobacco Plain Packaging*, at para 6.697.

[31] Appellate Body Report in *Australia – Tobacco Plain Packaging*, at para 6.655. The Panel's test requires a fact-dependent evaluation, which raises questions regarding the legitimate scope of state regulation under Article 20 and the viability of measures that, while not strictly 'necessary', nevertheless appear to be 'justifiable'. This is discussed further in A Maxwell, 'Plainly Justifiable? The World Trade Organization's Ruling on the Validity of Australia's "Plain Packaging" under Article 20 of the TRIPS Agreement', *AJPW* 14 (2019) 115.

TRIPS. This is the case in IP where 'TRIPS+ commitments' can be found in multiple FTAs. These commitments generally favour IP owners.

Such 'TRIPS+' provisions in FTAs can include provisions that encourage the recognition of a wider set of categories of trademark by including 'nontraditional' categories such as scent or sound,[32] and contain significant levels of detail on what systems governments should have in place to allow for the monitoring and enforcement of IP rights, including trademarks, within their jurisdictions.[33] The length of time that trademarks can be protected may also be extended beyond the TRIPS minimum of seven years (potentially renewable indefinitely)[34] – for example, to a minimum of ten years (renewable indefinitely) in the EU–Singapore FTA.[35]

At times, the expansion of benefits for IP owners included in FTAs are not accompanied by additional safeguards for the parties' regulatory autonomy as exist under the TRIPS with its attempts to balance coherent IP protection and other legitimate policy objectives.[36] The problem is exacerbated as FTAs do not only create a set of commitments for governments in abstract but also act as frameworks through which governments engage with each other (through committees and other joint bodies). Thus, FTAs not only create obligations but also provide avenues for governments to 'engage' and resolve disputes, potentially providing governments with the opportunity to represent a

---

[32] For example, Article 20.17 USMCA.

[33] For example, Articles 18.71–18.80 CPTPP.

[34] Article 18 TRIPS.

[35] Article 10.12 of the EU–Singapore FTA, by virtue of incorporating the Singapore Treaty on the Law of Trademarks 2006 (an international agreement to which the EU is not a party). Specifically, Article 13.5 provides the ten-year protection.

[36] H Grosse Ruse-Khan, 'From TRIPS to FTAs and Back: Re-conceptualising the Role of a Multilateral Intellectual Property Framework in a TRIPS-Plus World', *Netherlands Yearbook of International Law* (2017) 57.

more restrictive interpretation of the FTA's legal obligations in favour of their IP owners.

Crucially, once again, potential challenges to NCD prevention measures on IP and other trade grounds must be considered across multiple institutions, including the WTO and FTAs to which a government is a party, as well as international investment agreements, which we will turn to in the next chapter.

Placing TRIPS challenges within the wider trade and investment regime

The case of Chile

In the face of the rapid rise of obesity, especially among children and young people, Chile introduced a wide range of interventions to reduce the consumption of unhealthy food in 2016, specifically: (1) front-of-pack warning labels to indicate the high calorie, fat, salt, and sugar content; (2) extensive marketing restrictions, including the prohibition on the use of equity brand characters on packaging and the prohibition of packaged toys to promote unhealthy food; and (3) restrictions on where such food can be sold, specifically in schools.

Chile faced a range of legal challenges. In particular, the argument was repeatedly made that food marketing and product packaging regulation involving the use of trademarks interfered with the right to property, defined broadly to include IP. Beyond these arguments based on the Chilean Constitution heard in national courts, the government also had to address claims that such regulation infringed TRIPS in committees at the WTO.

This example demonstrates the point made in Chapter 1: that businesses, particularly large MNCs, can, and often will, simultaneously mount various legal challenges before a range of different courts and tribunals using the variety of legal bases at their disposal. While these bases will vary within different systems – depending on national constitutional arrangements as well as which FTAs and other agreements a government has concluded – we should not lose sight of the fact that different legal instruments, institutions, and commitments are all factors to carefully consider for governments with competent legal teams when regulating to prevent NCDs. This is especially important as the more effective a set of measures are, the more governments should expect, and therefore be prepared to defend, possible legal challenges to these measures.

7.7 Conclusions

In this chapter we have seen how IP rights and the protections they derive from TRIPS and FTAs are of particular importance for many NCD prevention policies, not least marketing, labelling, and other packaging requirements affecting the use of trademarks.

TRIPS requires Members to provide a level of protection for trademarks in their own national legal systems, but it also grants governments significant regulatory autonomy to restrict or limit those rights on public health and other legitimate grounds, provided that any encumbrance is appropriately justified. The importance of documenting public health policy decisions affecting trademarks used by the tobacco, alcohol, and food industries to promote the consumption of goods, services, and brands that harm public health should not be envisaged as a deterrent to legal challenge per se; it should instead be viewed as a reminder of the imperative for governments to engage in rigorous and transparent analysis relying on underpinning evidence.

EIGHT

International Investment Law and NCD Prevention

8.1 Introduction

In this chapter, we move away from international trade law to turn our attention to the other pillar of international economic law: international investment law (IIL) and how it may affect NCD prevention policies. Even though the corporate actors that engage with IIL to contest new NCD prevention measures are much the same as within the trade regime, IIL gives them different, potentially more powerful tools to pursue their objectives: IIL not only grants investors broad protections, but also provides mechanisms allowing them to directly challenge, and seek financial compensation from, governments rather than having to convince their own or another government to raise a dispute to protect their interests. As such, it empowers corporate actors more directly than international trade law does.

This is particularly relevant for the tobacco, alcohol, and food industries which have invested heavily around the world to establish their brands and strengthen their market position worldwide. Although such investment is now often associated with growing rates of NCDs, as discussed in Chapter 1, it can nonetheless be expected to continue. The more markets become regulated to protect public health, the more tobacco, alcohol, and food MNCs will seek to identify new, less regulated ones where they can grow and further their interests. This creates a tension for governments between their quest to attract FDI and their mandate to protect public health. These concerns are heightened where industry has resorted to IIL to recover the cost of product regulation or to pressure governments into abandoning such regulation rather than internalizing its cost.

Focusing specifically on the disputes Philip Morris initiated against Australia and Uruguay, and what they mean for NCD prevention, this chapter shows – here again – that governments have significant discretion to regulate the tobacco, alcohol, and food industries to protect public health on their territories. However, as we noted for international trade law, the public health objectives of certain measures do not, by themselves, shield governments from scrutiny; they must act within the constraints that IIL imposes upon them. After briefly introducing the IIL regime and how it interacts with public health (section 8.2), we consider the prohibition of discrimination (section 8.3), the obligation to accord fair and equitable treatment to foreign investors (section 8.4), and their protection against regulatory expropriation (section 8.5).

8.2 The international investment law regime and its relationship with public health

The IIL regime shares some characteristics with the international trade regime: it is a creation of public international law, it aims to promote economic growth (or at least defend certain economic interests), and IIL policy leads are based in trade or business ministries in most governments. However, IIL has a different history and important distinguishing features from international trade law, most notably the ways in which it empowers *private* actors to raise legal claims directly against governments before international tribunals: the so-called investor–state dispute settlement (ISDS).

8.2.1 Rationale

The origins of IIL can be traced back to the colonial expansion of Western powers. The underlying logic was to ensure that private actors from capital exporting states would be protected from unfriendly or unpredictable acts by the governments where their investment was based.[1] This logic evolved in the postwar period where IIL became the vehicle to encourage FDI within developing countries.

Although evidence of their positive effect is limited,[2] international investment agreements (IIAs) proliferated in the 1980s to increase FDI to promote economic growth and development by offering special protections for investors both:

- substantively, by granting them specific legal protections; and
- procedurally, by allowing them to challenge governments directly through ISDS and seek financial compensation, allowing them to sidestep national remedies and national courts.

8.2.2 The proliferation of IIAs and the characteristic features of international investment law

Whereas the WTO is a multilateral organization, there is no comparable multilateral body in IIL. Instead, the 'system' consists of multiple overlapping, often relatively short IIAs.

---

[1] See, in particular, A Anghie, 'The Evolution of International Law: Colonial and Postcolonial Realities' (2006) 27(5) *TWQ* 739; D Schneiderman, *Investment Law's Alibis: Colonialism, Imperialism, Debt and Development* (Cambridge: Cambridge University Press 2022); F Zarbiyev, ' "These Are My Principles. If You Don't Like Them I Have Others": On Justifications of Foreign Investment Protection under International Law', *JIEL* 26(3) (2023) 525.

[2] J Bonnitcha, L Poulsen, and M Waibel, *The Political Economy of the Investment Treaty Regime* (Oxford: Oxford University Press 2017).

Most are bilateral investment treaties (BITs).[3] More recently, regional, multi-party FTAs have also included comprehensive investment sections. Examples include CPTPP and the Comprehensive Economic and Trade Agreement between the EU and Canada (CETA). There are also some sectoral agreements, such as the Energy Charter Treaty which includes a section on international investment.[4]

IIAs are legally binding, not mere declarations of intent, and have been invoked in high-profile cases by private actors, not least the tobacco industry, to challenge national laws and policies likely to affect their interests. Worryingly, however, the nature and key features of IIAs are not always understood by governments before they conclude them.[5] IIL is indeed a particularly technical and complex area of law with unique features and potentially far-reaching implications. In particular, the financial consequences of investment arbitration for respondent states, both in terms of the damages awarded and the cost of the arbitration process itself, may detract from important public interest objectives, including health protection. Developing countries are particularly prone to a 'race to the bottom' to attract FDI, as they may find themselves more vulnerable to threats from powerful MNCs that have invested within their borders. Higher-income countries are not immune from the impact of IIL on national policy making either. Raising awareness of IIL and its implications for states considering IIAs is therefore crucial so that governments can protect themselves more effectively from successful challenges to NCD prevention measures both at an early stage when such agreements are negotiated and later on in the policy process when they are invoked by foreign investors against a host state before an arbitral tribunal.

---

[3] Currently 2,834 signed BITs, of which 2,223 are in force.

[4] Information on the various types of IIAs can be found on the investment policy hub of the UN Trade and Development (UNCTAD): https://investmentpolicy.unctad.org/international-investment-agreements

[5] M Sattorova, *The Impact of Investment Treaty Law on Host States* (Oxford: Hart Publishing, 2018).

8.2.3 The structure of IIAs, key terms, and dispute settlement

IIAs have been standardized and tend to have a similar structure. Understanding their specific language, content, and context is nonetheless essential to assess the relationship between IIL and public health, and to evaluate concerns about possible limitations on the state's NCD prevention strategies.

Generally, IIAs consist of three parts: definitions; standards of protection granted to investors; and dispute settlement mechanisms.

Definitions are crucial to delineate the scope of application of IIAs, not least those of 'investor' and 'investment'.

IIL protects private investors, broadly defined to include natural and legal persons (that is, both people and companies). As protection is given only to foreign nationals (that is, nationals of other IIA parties), investors must demonstrate that they have the requisite nationality.

An abusive change of nationality by a corporation for the mere purpose of accessing international arbitration is increasingly being rejected by arbitral tribunals. For example, when Philip Morris Asia challenged the compatibility of Australia tobacco plain packaging legislation with IIL based on the Hong Kong/Australia BIT in 2011, the Tribunal found that it had incorporated in Hong Kong solely with the aim of gaining access to the BIT and its dispute resolution instruments. The Tribunal therefore denied jurisdiction and held the claim to be inadmissible. Consequently, while the case attracted a lot of attention and required that Australia incur high litigation costs,[6]

---

[6] Reportedly, Australia spent nearly $40 million defending its world-first plain packaging laws against Philip Morris Asia. See Gareth Hutchens and Christopher Knaus, 'Revealed: $39m Cost of Defending Australia's Tobacco Plain Packaging Laws' (*The Guardian*, 1 July 2018), https://www.theguardian.com/business/2018/jul/02/revealed-39m-cost-of-defending-australias-tobacco-plain-packaging-laws

the Tribunal did not engage with the substance of the claim.[7]

Investment, another key concept at the heart of IIL, is also defined broadly. IIAs often cover physical assets (for example, factories, mines, or longstanding businesses), as well as IP, portfolio investment, and shares. In other words, IIAs generally cover both tangible and intangible property. This is why restrictions imposed on the use of trademarks, particularly on tobacco products, have given rise to claims under IIL. Similar claims could arise for measures intended to limit the consumption of alcohol and unhealthy food, such as the imposition of alcohol health warnings,[8] or FoPNL.[9]

The BIT between Switzerland and Uruguay (1988)

Article 1 Definitions

For the purposes of this Agreement: [...]

(2) The term 'investments' shall include every kind of assets and particularly:
   a) movable and immovable property as well as any other rights in rem, such as charges on real estate, mortgages, liens, pledges;
   b) shares, certificates or other kinds of participation in companies;
   c) money claims and any entitlements of economic value;
   d) copyrights, industrial property rights (such as patents of inventions, utility models, industrial designs or models, trade or service marks, trade names, indications of source or appellation of origin), know-how and goodwill;

---

[7] *Philip Morris Asia Ltd v The Commonwealth of Australia*, UNCITRAL, PCA Case No. 2012–12, Award on Jurisdiction and Admissibility (17 December 2015).

[8] A Mitchell and P O'Brien, 'If One Thai Bottle Should Accidentally Fall: Health Information, Alcohol Labelling and International Investment Law', *JWIT* 21(5) (2020) 674.

[9] M Campbell, 'Chile: Front-of-Package Warning Labels and Food Marketing', *Journal of Law, Medicine & Ethics* 50(2) (2022) 298.

> e) concessions under public law, including concessions to search for, extract or exploit natural resources as well as all other rights given by law, by contract or by decision of a public entity in accordance with the law.

Investments also need to be made in the territory of the host state, incur a certain risk, involve a commitment of resources, be of a certain duration.[10] How strictly these tests are applied will depend on the tribunal. In *Philip Morris v Uruguay*, for example, Uruguay objected that Philip Morris' activities were not an investment because they were not assisting Uruguay's development (in fact, the opposite). The Tribunal disagreed, holding that an investment could prove useful or not for a host state without losing its quality as an investment.[11] As will be discussed later on, the type of investment becomes relevant when determining the limits of the protection granted to investors, rather than when defining the scope of an IIA. Therefore, provided that trademarks have been exploited in the marketplace for a reasonable time, they will be protected investments under IIL, particularly when the relevant IIA expressly includes IP rights in its definition of investment.

8.2.4 Dispute settlement

After identifying the substantive standards protecting foreign investors and their investment, IIAs contain a dispute resolution clause, which generally requires that disputes be resolved by binding international arbitration. Disputes can be inter-state

---

[10] The so-called 'Salini test': *Salini Costruttori S.p.A. and Italstrade S.p.A. v Kingdom of Morocco* [I], ICSID Case No. ARB/00/4.

[11] Even though considerations related to the development of the host State are relevant, they do not become 'a constitutional element of the concept of investment' (at paras 208 and 209).

but, unusually for international law, most IIAs also grant the right to foreign investors to challenge the laws and regulations of a host state which they deem to be incompatible with their provisions. Disputes against a host state are heard by panels of (customarily) three arbitrators chosen by the parties: one by the investor, one by the host state, and one selected by agreement of the parties or, failing that, by an external appointing authority.

Awards are binding and cannot be appealed.[12] As such, ISDS amounts to a transfer of adjudicative authority from national courts to arbitral tribunals: under most IIAs, states have waived their sovereign immunity, giving arbitrators a comprehensive jurisdiction over regulatory disputes. This, in turn, raises the question whether public health can be effectively protected within a framework aimed primarily at protecting private interests.

ISDS has faced growing criticism, as it has increasingly been used to resolve disputes related to public goods, such as environmental protection, sovereign debt, and public health, which call for greater public scrutiny. Critics argue that ISDS lacks transparency. Confidentiality is one of the main features of ISDS proceedings, and while some proceedings do become public, the lack of certainty is problematic – especially as disputes may deal directly with public policy matters. Moreover, as the only duty bearers are states, while investors only hold rights, the system lends itself to a small group of powerful players (those with significant financial means). These criticisms have generated ample discussion, to which the ISDS system has attempted to respond, as will be discussed next.[13]

---

[12] Though there is a limited ability to annul some awards where the Tribunal was not properly constituted, the Tribunal manifestly exceeded its powers, there was corruption on the part of a member of the Tribunal, there was a serious departure from a fundamental rule of procedure, or the Award failed to state the reasons on which it was based (Article 52 of the ICSID Convention).

[13] For example, United Nations Convention on Transparency in Treaty-Based Investor-State Arbitration 2014, and subsequent ongoing work by the UNCITRAL Working Group III on Investor-State Dispute Settlement Reform.

8.2.5 Instrumentalizing the large number of, and differences between, IIAs

As mentioned previously, there are several differences between IIAs. Two important ones should be mentioned at this stage:

- first, some IIAs require an investor to have attempted to resolve its concerns in national courts and exhaust local remedies first (for example, over 18 or 24 months) before it can resort to international arbitration, while others do not;
- second, the nationality of a foreign investor is defined in the IIA. Some IIAs define the eligible investors with reference to the place of incorporation, whereas others include the additional requirement of a seat and substantial economic activities. Therefore, while some IIAs broadly define the nationality of investors (and therefore whether they can rely on the specific treaty), simply requiring incorporation in that market, others require a meaningful or genuine link, including the establishment of its headquarters.

As a result of these differences, private actors play an elaborate game of 'treaty shopping', identifying which IIA offers the greatest protection for their investment and has the most favourable dispute settlement provisions.

The lack of a clear overarching system for dispute settlement also means that these ad hoc arbitration tribunals need not interpret the law consistently with each other, although they often draw on each other's decisions. This leads to some legal uncertainty that can, in turn, generate anxiety and creates *doubt* over the content and scope of the obligations that bind governments when they consider public health regulation. This doubt is instrumentalized by private actors who exploit the risk-aversion of governments and lobby for the withdrawal or the watering-down of the envisaged measures long before any formal legal challenge materializes.

This strategy is even more effective as the remedies granted to investors against host states can be extremely high when they lose IIL disputes. Whereas the WTO Member's duty is to comply or face retaliation under international trade law, investors commonly receive financial compensation under IIL. Awards against host states can be eye-watering[14] and are, in theory, readily enforceable against host state property. This exerts a potentially powerful deterrent effect which may lead to regulatory chill on government policy.[15] Additionally, investors may be able to rely on the award from the arbitral tribunal in national courts for enforcement where they are treated as orders of those courts. This co-opts the enforcement capacity of national courts to secure compliance for traditionally less enforceable international commitments.

8.2.6 NCD prevention and international investment law

IIL and health have become increasingly related, raising the core question of the extent to which states have discretion to regulate on public health grounds when such regulation may affect foreign investors. There could indeed be tension between the regulatory space that states must retain to protect health

---

[14] For example, the compensation awards for unlawful expropriation were $1.7 billion in *Occidental v Ecuador* (2012) ICSID Case No ARB/06/11 and $8.7 billion in *ConocoPhillips v Venezuela* (2018) (although the actual amounts recovered are considerably less).

[15] See G Van Harten, *Sold Down the Yangtze* (Burlington ON: IIAPP, 2015). On regulatory chill, IIL and NCD prevention, see M Sattorova, 'Investment Protection Agreements, Regulatory Chill, and National Measures on Childhood Obesity Prevention', in A Garde, J Curtis and O De Schutter, *Ending Childhood Obesity: A Challenge at the Crossroads of International Economic and Human Rights Law* (Cheltenham: Edward Elgar, 2020), pp 175–179; and O Vytiaganets, 'Smoking Chills? Tobacco Regulatory Chill, Foreign Investment, and the NCD Crisis in the Post-Soviet Space: A Case Study from Ukraine', *JWIT* 20 (2020) 753.

as an important public interest and the protection of private investment from unlawful state interference.

Overall, arbitral tribunals have increasingly acknowledged the need to afford host states sufficient policy space to protect public health and other legitimate interests:

> As a matter of general international law, a non-discriminatory regulation for a public purpose, which is enacted in accordance with due process and which affects, inter alia, a foreign investor or investment is not deemed expropriatory and compensable unless specific commitment had been given by the regulating government to the then putative foreign investor contemplating investment that the government would refrain from such regulation.[16]

Such an approach is manifest in several high-profile public health cases. For example, in *Methanex v US* (2015) – a North American Free Trade Agreement (NAFTA) case concerning the marketing and distribution of methanol – Methanex claimed damages worth $970 million for partial expropriation of its investment, as well as denial of fair and equitable treatment (FET) and national treatment. The Tribunal dismissed all claims, ruling that the sales ban rested on scientific evidence and due process, and had been adopted in a transparent manner. Methanex was ordered to pay around $4 million towards the host state's legal and arbitration costs.[17]

The tension between state regulatory autonomy to prevent NCDs and the obligation of abiding by IIL came to the fore in the seminal *Philip Morris v Uruguay* decision on tobacco control where due regard was given to the states' right to regulate.[18]

---

[16] *Methanex v US* (2005), at para 287.
[17] See also *Chemtura Corporation v Canada* (2009) PCS Case No. 2008-01.
[18] *Philip Morris Brands Sàrl, Philip Morris Products S.A. and Abal Hermanos S.A. v Oriental Republic of Uruguay*, ICSID Case No. ARB/10/7, Award (8 July 2016).

Philip Morris v Uruguay (2016): an introduction

As a country with 'one of Latin America's highest rate of smokers',[19] Uruguay enacted strong anti-smoking legislation, including: (1) a requirement that cigarette brands sell only under a single package or variant (the so-called 'Single Presentation Requirement'); and (2) a requirement that the health warnings affixed on cigarette packages increase from 50 per cent to 80 per cent of the surface of the packages (the so-called '80/80 Regulation').

Relying on the BIT signed between Uruguay and Switzerland, Philip Morris challenged the measures on several grounds, including that they resulted in partial expropriation of investment and violated the FET standard. On this basis, it requested that the Tribunal order Uruguay to either withdraw the challenged regulations or refrain from applying them against their investments, or, in the alternative, award it damages of at least $22.267 million, plus compound interest, as well as the firm's fees and expenses, including legal fees, incurred in connection with the arbitration.[20]

The Tribunal, by a majority of two to one, dismissed Philip Morris' claims in their entirety and upheld the legality of the challenged public health measures. It also ordered Philip Morris to bear all arbitral costs and to pay Uruguay $7 million as partial reimbursement of its legal expenses.

Importantly, the parties did not dispute that smoking constituted a serious health risk; rather, the claimant founded its case on the assertion that Uruguay's measures constituted a violation of the IP rights it owned and therefore constituted indirect expropriation of its investment in violation of the BIT. However, the Tribunal ruled that there was not even a prima facie case of indirect expropriation by the 80/80 measure, as the brand's distinctive elements were still recognizable on cigarette packs.[21] Nor was there indirect expropriation

---

[19] *Philip Morris Brands Sàrl, Philip Morris Products S.A. and Abal Hermanos S.A. v Oriental Republic of Uruguay*, ICSID Case No. ARB/10/7, Award (8 July 2016), at para 75.

[20] *Philip Morris v Uruguay*, at para 12.

[21] *Philip Morris v Uruguay*, at para 276.

by the Single Presentation Requirement, as it did not cause a 'substantial deprivation' of the investment as a whole.[22] As the Tribunal highlighted, as long the investment as a whole retains sufficient value following the implementation of the contested measures,[23] there is no indirect expropriation.[24] In this case, the claimant had not demonstrated any damage by the Single Presentation Requirement. In any event, the Tribunal found that there was 'a consistent trend in favour of differentiating the exercise of policy powers from indirect expropriation' and whether a measure amounted to expropriation depended on the nature and purpose of the actions of the state.[25]

The Tribunal also rejected the claim that Uruguay had breached the FET standard. It ruled that the Single Presentation Requirement was not arbitrary and that it presented a reasonable 'attempt to address a real public health concern'.[26] Similarly, it held that the 80/80 Regulation was a 'reasonable measure adopted in good faith', supported by a strong scientific consensus on the dangers of tobacco.[27]

The importance of this case for our purposes cannot be understated. It clearly recognizes that states can regulate and even refuse to admit investments for public health reasons.[28] Other such decisions are likely to follow as the regulation of the tobacco, alcohol, and food industries becomes more widespread.

The following sections discuss the arguments most frequently invoked by foreign investors against host states, introduced here in *Philip Morris v Uruguay*, and the pitfalls that national regulators need to avoid, focusing specifically on IIA provisions on non-discrimination, compensation for expropriation, and FET.

---

[22] *Philip Morris v Uruguay*, at para 284.
[23] Interestingly, the Tribunal noted that Philip Morris' business had, overall, grown more profitable in the period after the implementation of the Single Presentation Requirement: *Philip Morris v Uruguay*, at para 284.
[24] *Philip Morris v Uruguay*, at para 286.
[25] *Philip Morris v Uruguay*, at para 295.
[26] *Philip Morris v Uruguay*, at paras 409–410.
[27] *Philip Morris v Uruguay*, at para 420.
[28] *Philip Morris v Uruguay*, at para 291.

Before doing so, we will note that IIAs increasingly include provisions dealing specifically with public health. These provisions have begun to be introduced as a response to arbitral awards applying investor protections with insufficient care for public policy outcomes.[29] Often framed as 'clarifying' the scope of investment protections, such provisions reaffirm and specifically outline the regulatory powers of states in public health and other related concerns, seeking to address the criticism that IIL may be unbalanced and favour investors. The right to regulate provision of CETA is an illustrative example.

Article 8.9 CETA

1. For the purpose of this Chapter, the Parties reaffirm their right to regulate within their territories to achieve legitimate policy objectives, such as the protection of public health, safety, the environment or public morals, social or consumer protection, or the promotion and protection of cultural diversity.
2. For greater certainty, the mere fact that a Party regulates, including through a modification to its laws, in a manner which negatively affects an investment or interferes with an investor's expectations, including its expectations of profits, does not amount to a breach of an obligation under this Section.

Whether or not a host state can rely on an explicit right-to-regulate clause, governments have significant scope to regulate on public health and related grounds. If they anticipate potential IIL challenges, they may either avert them altogether or defend them successfully if such challenges are forthcoming. This is subject to the important caveat made earlier that the highly fragmented IIL landscape, with its multiplicity of IIAs and lack

---

[29] For example, *PL Holdings S.à.r.l. v Republic of Poland*, SCC Case No. V 2014/163 and *Continental Casualty Company v The Argentine Republic*, ICSID Case No. ARB/03/9.

of centralized arbitration system, creates an unavoidable degree of legal uncertainty.

8.3 Non-discrimination in international investment law

IIL includes key non-discrimination requirements. However, and very importantly, non-discrimination in IIL does not mean equivalent treatment as in international trade law; by their very nature, foreign investors can – and do – receive preferential treatment compared to national investors under IIAs. A core element of IIL is to encourage investment by reducing the risk for investors from governments' decisions which run against core 'standards' of treatment, as will be discussed further later on. While WTO law applies – in most instances – to all WTO Members, IIL commitments vary in both content and enforcement mechanisms across IIAs. Here, we identify certain common features: MFN, national treatment, and FET.

8.3.1 MFN

As with international trade law, IIL also includes MFN commitments, as the following example illustrates.

The BIT between Switzerland and Uruguay (1988)

Article 3 Protection and Treatment of Investments

1. Each Contracting Party shall protect within its territory investments made in accordance with its legislation by investors of the other Contracting Party and shall not impair by unreasonable or discriminatory measures the management, maintenance, use, enjoyment, extension, sale and, should it so happen, liquidation of such investments. In particular, each Contracting Party shall issue the necessary authorizations mentioned in Article 2, paragraph (2) of this Agreement.
2. Each Contracting Party shall ensure fair and equitable treatment within its territory of the investments of the investors of the other

Contracting Party. This treatment shall not be less favourable than that granted by each Contracting Party to investments made within its territory by its own investors, or than that granted by each Contracting Party to the investments made within its territory by investors of the most favoured nation, if this latter treatment is more favourable.

3. The treatment of the most favoured nation shall not apply to privileges which either Contracting Party accords to investors of a third State because of its membership in, or association with a free trade area, a customs union or a common market.

4. The treatment of the most favoured nation shall neither be applicable to advantages which either Contracting Party grants to investors of a third State by virtue of a double taxation agreement or other agreements regarding matters of taxation.

Under an IIA, a government may be required to provide the same benefits to an investor. However, while MFN is a core pillar of the multilateral trade regime, its influence is more variable in IIL for two key reasons. First, MFN provisions under IIAs will often have exclusions. For example, they may not apply to government procurement or taxation measures, which could leave an investor frustrated that the government is preferring one of their competitors from a third country through tax incentives. Second, the interpretation of MFN provisions under IIAs has been inconsistent. In some disputes, investors have successfully argued that an IIA with limited protections for them should be improved by importing better protections through the MFN provision, such as a more generous method for calculating expropriation. Saying that better protections given to other investors under *another* IIA is an advantage they should be able to receive potentially expands the scope of the IIA that a government negotiated with one specific partner (and their companies) in mind.[30] Some tribunals have gone even further and applied it to

---

[30] For example, *Pope & Talbot Inc. v The Government of Canada*, UNCITRAL (2000).

dispute settlement: as was noted earlier, the requirements to gain access to arbitration differ between IIAs. One may require the investor to use national courts to enforce its rights for a period of 18 or 24 months before it can access an international arbitral tribunal, while another may include no such obligation. Through using the MFN clause, some investors have successfully argued that they are able to rely on the more favourable IIA because another treaty has no such requirement, they should be able to 'jump' straight to arbitration.[31] *Uncertainty* thus becomes a major challenge for a government.

One might look at this situation and take heart: it is unclear, and in many cases, investors were not able to 'pull' in additional protections from the MFN provision under the IIA.[32] However, as foreshadowed earlier, the activities of private actors are extensive and well resourced, while governments tend to be cautious and risk-averse. A well-drafted letter from a high-end New York, London, Geneva, or Paris law firm can cast enough doubt to tip the *internal* balance between ministries of health, finance, and commerce.

8.3.2 National treatment

The second 'pillar' of the non-discrimination pillar in trade law – national treatment – exists in IIL too: foreign investors can be treated no less favourably than national investors in like circumstances. Importantly, however, they can receive better treatment than domestic investors, but not worse. CETA again provides a helpful illustrative example of this.

---

[31] For example, *Emilio Agustín Maffezini v The Kingdom of Spain*, ICSID Case No. ARB/97/7; *Siemens A.G. v Argentine Republic* (ICSID Case ARB/02/8). Decision on Jurisdiction, 3 August 2004.

[32] For a useful discussion, see JP Villablanca Gutiérrez, 'The Use of MFN Clauses in Investment Arbitration: The Problem of Importation', *Journal of International Dispute Settlement* 15(3) (2024) 424.

Article 8.6 CETA

1. Each Party shall accord to an investor of the other Party and to a covered investment, treatment no less favourable than the treatment it accords, in like situations to its own investors and to their investments with respect to the establishment, acquisition, expansion, conduct, operation, management, maintenance, use, enjoyment and sale or disposal of their investments in its territory.
2. The treatment accorded by a Party under paragraph 1 means, with respect to a government in Canada other than at the federal level, treatment no less favourable than the most favourable treatment accorded, in like situations, by that government to investors of Canada in its territory and to investments of such investors.
3. The treatment accorded by a Party under paragraph 1 means, with respect to a government of or in a Member State of the European Union, treatment no less favourable than the most favourable treatment accorded, in like situations, by that government to investors of the EU in its territory and to investments of such investors.

The key question is whether foreign investments are regulated because they entail certain health risks or whether they are regulated because they are foreign investments. A host state cannot favour its home-based companies over foreign companies merely by virtue of nationality. For example, in the *Marvin Feldman Karpa* case, involving taxes of tobacco products, the Tribunal ruled that measures allowing rebates only to producers violated the principle of non-discrimination.[33]

As in international trade law, violations of national treatment in IIL can stem either from explicit discriminatory measures (in law) or from measures that discriminate in practice (de facto), with the focus being on the discriminatory effect of the measure. Moreover, the measure itself need not be a specific

---

[33] *Marvin Roy Feldman Karpa v United Mexican States*, ICSID Case No. ARB(AF)/99/1. See also *S.D. Myers, Inc. v Government of Canada*, UNCITRAL.

regulatory provision; it can also be the manner in which the government is implementing or applying a measure or a set of measures.[34] Foreign investors therefore benefit from a potentially broad protection.[35]

However, in the context of public health and NCD prevention, there are some important caveats, specifically regarding the way in which the basis of the discrimination is understood. For example, CPTPP includes an interpretative note clarifying the interpretation of 'like circumstances':

The phrase 'in like circumstances' ensures that comparisons are made only with respect to investors or investments on the basis of relevant characteristics. This is a fact-specific inquiry requiring consideration of the totality of the circumstances, as reflected in paragraphs 4 and 5. Such circumstances include not only competition in the relevant business or economic sectors, but also such circumstances as the applicable legal and regulatory frameworks *and whether the differential treatment is based on legitimate public welfare objectives*. Accordingly, the Parties agreed to include a new footnote in the text: 'For greater certainty, whether treatment is accorded in "like circumstances" depends on the totality of the circumstances, including whether the relevant treatment distinguishes between investors or investments on the basis of legitimate public welfare objectives.'[36]

---

[34] See A Bjorklund, 'National Treatment', in A Reinisch (ed.), *Standards of Investment Protection* (Oxford: Oxford University Press, 2008), pp 29–58.

[35] Additionally, in some cases, IIAs may also include national treatment protections for investors before they are established in the host state (so-called pre-establishment protections). These are often subject to sectoral and substantive limitations, but can also increase the protections available to MNCs. See, for example, Article 3(1) of the US Model BIT (2012).

[36] Drafters' Note on Interpretation of 'in Like Circumstances' under Article 9.4 (National Treatment) and Article 9.5 (Most-Favoured-Nation Treatment). Emphasis added.

This shows the more recent practice under IIAs where governments have sought to 'clarify' the appropriate scope of protection for investors, and that where one investor, even if foreign, is subject to differential treatment, where this is based on 'legitimate public welfare objectives', such as public health protection, they are not considered in like circumstances and therefore the national treatment principle does not apply. This is, of course, the case where these legitimate public welfare objectives provide the real basis for the differential treatment, in the absence of disguised discrimination.

Beyond MFN and national treatment, non-discrimination also plays an important role in the evaluation of whether foreign investors have been treated fairly and equitably.

8.4 Fair and equitable treatment

The FET standard is a cornerstone of IIL and the most frequently invoked argument by investors challenging governments in ISDS. It requires that foreign investors be accorded a minimum standard treatment, historically understood as 'treatment of an alien … [that amounts] to an outrage, to bad faith, to wilful neglect of duty, or to an insufficiency of governmental action so far short of international standards that every reasonable and impartial man would readily recognize its insufficiency'.[37]

8.4.1 The scope of FET

The *exact* contours of the FET standard are not easy to define. The standard tends to be vague and open-ended, which leaves ample scope for (potentially diverging) interpretation and inconsistency in arbitral practice. This is compounded by the fact that the FET standard can differ significantly from one IIA to another. The definition of FET is indeed treaty-specific,

---

[37] *L.F.H. Neer and Pauline Neer (U.S.A.) v United Mexican States* (1926), RIAA, Volume IV, pp 60–66, 15 October 1926, para 4.

and both the wording and the specific circumstances of each case matter in determining the outcome of a dispute. The examples in the following box demonstrate how different two FET provisions can be.

Example 1: Article 3(2) of the BIT between Switzerland and Uruguay (1988)

Each Contracting Party shall ensure fair and equitable treatment within its territory of the investments of the investors of the other Contracting Party. This treatment shall not be less favourable than that granted by each Contracting Party to investments made within its territory by its own investors, or than that granted by each Contracting Party to the investments made within its territory by investors of the most favoured nation, if this latter treatment is more favourable.

Example 2: Article 8.10 of CETA between Canada and the European Union

1. Each Party shall accord in its territory to covered investments of the other Party and to investors with respect to their covered investments fair and equitable treatment and full protection and security in accordance with paragraphs 2 through 7.
2. A Party breaches the obligation of fair and equitable treatment referenced in paragraph 1 if a measure or series of measures constitutes:
   a) denial of justice in criminal, civil or administrative proceedings;
   b) fundamental breach of due process, including a fundamental breach of transparency, in judicial and administrative proceedings;
   c) manifest arbitrariness;
   d) targeted discrimination on manifestly wrongful grounds, such as gender, race or religious belief;
   e) abusive treatment of investors, such as coercion, duress and harassment; or
   f) a breach of any further elements of the fair and equitable treatment obligation adopted by the Parties in accordance with paragraph 3 of this Article.
3. The Parties shall regularly, or upon request of a Party, review the content of the obligation to provide fair and equitable treatment ...

4. When applying the above fair and equitable treatment obligation, the Tribunal may take into account whether a Party made a specific representation to an investor to induce a covered investment, that created a legitimate expectation, and upon which the investor relied in deciding to make or maintain the covered investment, but that the Party subsequently frustrated.

It is not possible to review existing differences across the vast number of IIAs in greater detail here.[38] Instead, the rest of this section extracts core common elements of the FET standard, as interpreted in decisions directly relevant to public health and NCD prevention.

When called upon to interpret the FET standard, tribunals have examined issues relating to non-discrimination, the legitimacy of the challenged measures, the stability and the protection of the legitimate expectations of investors, the transparency of the domestic legal frameworks, procedural compliance and due process and issues of good faith.

It is clear from the wording of these two examples that the prohibition against discrimination by host states against foreign investors is an important element of the FET standard. In particular, host states should provide investors in regulatory and legal proceedings with due process (which includes, among other elements, protection from discrimination). This could mean, for instance, that the investor should be given a fair opportunity to present their case before an impartial tribunal or challenge a regulation.

The case law provides answers to two main sets of questions, around which we have structured the rest of this section: whether the challenged measures are legitimate and not arbitrary; and whether the legitimate expectations of the foreign investors have been met.

---

[38] For a detailed analysis, see M Paparinskis, *The International Minimum Standard and Fair and Equitable Treatment* (Oxford: Oxford University Press, 2013).

8.4.2 The legitimacy of the challenged measures

In claims that specific measures are arbitrary and therefore unlawful under IIL, arbitral tribunals tend to define 'arbitrariness' as a 'wilful disregard of due process of law, an act which shocks, or at least surprises, a sense of juridical propriety'.[39] In particular, arbitral tribunals consider whether a host state's conduct is reasonably related to the legitimate policy objective it pursues, as was the case for the measures at stake in the challenge Philip Morris mounted against Uruguay.[40]

To this effect, tribunals consider the evidence underpinning the challenged measures. For example, in *Methanex v US*, the Tribunal highlighted the 'serious, objective and scientific approach to a complex problem' which California had adopted. It concluded that no violation of the FET standard had occurred, as the policy decision taken by California was motivated by an honest belief held in good faith and based on scientific findings which California had implemented after public hearings, testimony, and peer review. The Tribunal also highlighted that there was no evidence that California was trying to favour the US ethanol industry or other companies or injure methanol producers (that is, there was no discrimination).[41]

Similarly, in *Chemtura v Canada*, the Tribunal highlighted that the relevant agency had initiated a special review out of 'legitimate regulatory concerns' and in accordance with Canada's international obligations. As such, Canada had not acted unfairly towards foreign investors. Importantly, the Tribunal also clarified that it was not for it to judge whether

---

[39] *Elettronica Sicula S.p.A. (ELSI) (United States of America v Italy)*, ICJ Reports 1989, p 15, at para 128.

[40] *Philip Morris Brands Sàrl, Philip Morris Products S.A. and Abal Hermanos S.A. v Oriental Republic of Uruguay*, ICSID Case No. ARB/10/7 (formerly *FTR Holding SA, Philip Morris Products S.A. and Abal Hermanos S.A. v Oriental Republic of Uruguay*).

[41] *Methanex Corporation v USA*, Final Award on Jurisdiction and Merits (2005).

the scientific results of the special review were correct and adequate; its role was only to review how and why the special review had been initiated. It concluded that Chemtura's claim was devoid of any factual basis or legal foundation.[42]

In *Philip Morris v Uruguay*, the Tribunal considered several elements to conclude that Uruguay's measures were legitimate and not arbitrary: the purpose of the measures challenged; their relationship with the objectives they pursued and whether they were reasonable; the evidence regarding their effectiveness; Uruguay's international obligations under the FCTC; and whether Uruguay had acted in good faith. Regarding Uruguay's legal obligations under the FCTC specifically, the Tribunal noted that there was sufficient evidence based on the FCTC and that Uruguay therefore did not have to gather further evidence to establish the reasonableness of the contested measures. As in *Chemtura*, the Tribunal also noted that its role was limited to reviewing whether there was a manifest lack of reasons for the legislation before concluding that the Single Presentation Requirement was 'a reasonable measure, not an arbitrary, grossly unfair, unjust, discriminatory or a disproportionate measure'.[43] As for the 80/80 Regulation, it specifically noted that it was supported by a strong scientific consensus on the dangers of tobacco:

> 418. In the Tribunal's view, the present case concerns a legislative policy decision taken against the background of a strong scientific consensus as to the lethal effects of tobacco. Substantial deference is due in that regard to national authorities' decisions as to the measures which should be taken to address an acknowledged and major public health problem. The fair and equitable treatment

---

[42] *Chemtura Corporation (Formerly Crompton Corporation) v Government of Canada*, PCA Case No. 2008–01.

[43] *Philip Morris v Uruguay*, at para 410.

standard is not a justiciable standard of good government, and the tribunal is not a court of appeal. Article 3(2) does not dictate, for example, that a 50% health warning requirement is fair whereas an 80% requirement is not. In one sense an 80% requirement is arbitrary in that it could have been 60% or 75% or for that matter 85% or 90%. *Some* limit had to be set, and the balance to be struck between conflicting considerations was very largely a matter for the government.

419. In the end, the question is whether the 80 limit in fact set was entirely lacking in justification or wholly disproportionate, due account being taken of the legitimate underlying aim – viz., to make utterly clear to consumers the serious risks of smoking. The Claimants did not object to the *content* of the warnings, which reflected the scientific consensus of the different harmful effects of continued smoking, but only to their size increase to 80% with respect to the previously-accepted 50% size. How a government requires the acknowledged health risks of products, such as tobacco, to be communicated to the persons at risk, is a matter of public policy, to be left to the appreciation of the regulatory authority.

420. In short, the 80/80 Regulation was a reasonable measure adopted in good faith to implement an obligation assumed by the State under the FCTC. It was not an arbitrary, grossly unfair, unjust, discriminatory or a disproportionate measure, in particular given its relatively minor impact on Abal's business. The Tribunal concludes that its adoption was not in breach of Article 3(2) of the BIT.

As this excerpt suggests, the level of evidence required is related to the nature of the obligation on the government. Therefore, and as already mentioned earlier, the specific wording of commitments under IIAs must always be carefully investigated.

The Tribunal award confirms that the FCTC and the IIL regimes can indeed be reconciled, and that states do not have to accept unnecessary limits on their regulatory power. Although arbitral tribunals cannot issue a finding of compliance or non-compliance with the FCTC, as this ultimately falls outside their mandate, they can evaluate the legitimacy and good faith character of a given regulatory measure in light of international objective standards such as those enshrined in the FCTC.[44]

This is even more the case as the Tribunal also relied on the concept of 'margin of appreciation' first used in decisions of the European Court of Human Rights to highlight the deference that states must be granted in policy matters such as public health protection:

> The Tribunal agrees with the Respondent that the 'margin of appreciation' is not limited to the context of the ECHR but applies equally to claims arising under BITs, at least in contexts such as public health. The responsibility for public health measures rests with the government and investment tribunals should pay great deference to governmental judgments of national needs in matters such as the protection of public health. In such cases respect is due to the discretionary exercise of sovereign power, not made irrationally and not exercised in bad faith … involving many complex factors. As held by another investment tribunal, '[t]he sole inquiry for the Tribunal … is whether or not there was a manifest lack of reasons for the legislation … the responsibility for public health measures rest with the government and investment tribunals should pay great deference to government judgments of national needs in matters such as the protection of public health'.[45]

---

[44] On the reconciliation of conflicting interests in IIL, see V Vadi, *Public Health in International Investment Law and Arbitration* (Abingdon: Routledge, 2012), pp 163–188.

[45] *Philip Morris v Uruguay*, at para 399.

As colleagues have noted, the Tribunal's award in *Philip Morris v Uruguay* provides a possible analytical approach under IIL to any product labelling requirement adopted for a public policy purpose, such as alcohol health warning labels or FoPNL or marketing restrictions on product packaging.[46]

8.4.3 The legitimate expectations of foreign investors

An investor affected by NCD prevention measures might also argue that these measures breach the FET standard by running against the investor's legitimate expectations.[47] It should be noted that some BIT clauses on FET will specifically refer to such expectations, as the example of CETA Article 8.10 demonstrates (see paragraph 4).

The concept of 'legitimate expectation' is often considered in the assessment of FET. Its roots are in domestic law where – in general terms – a party is entitled to rely on a reasonable expectation, subject to certain conditions. In the investment context, the purpose of this right for investors is to ensure that their reasonable expectations of certain conditions for their investment remain stable, thus allowing them to realize a return on such investment. In short, where a state creates reasonable expectations on the part of an investor to rely on its conduct, the failure by the state to honour those expectations could cause a detriment to the investor, thus giving rise to a claim in IIL.[48]

---

[46] A Mitchell and P O'Brien, 'If One Thai Bottle Should Accidentally Fall: Health Information, Alcohol Labelling and International Investment Law', *JWIT* 21 (2020) 674; M Campbell, 'NCD Prevention and International Investment Law in Latin America: Chile's Experience in Preventing Obesity and Unhealthy Diets', *JWIT* 21 (2020) 781.

[47] For example, *Saluka Investments B.V. v The Czech Republic* (2006) UNCITRAL. Partial Award, para 305, noting that the FET standard balances the right of the host State to exercise its regulatory authority in the public interest with the 'legitimate expectations' of foreign investors.

[48] For example, *International Thunderbird Gaming Corporation v Mexico*, Award, IIC 136 (2006) Ad Hoc Tribunal (UNCITRAL).

This may raise concerns for regulating governments. After all, investors may well invest in a specific market precisely because of the existing regulatory environment. Just as the international trade law system is interested in providing a level of certainty for economic actors to better take long-term decisions, so does IIL seek to provide a level of predictability for investors. However, this does not mean that an investor can claim that it expected no change in the regulatory environment. Instead, the government must have created a reasonable expectation of such a situation.

National regulators should be mindful that FET requires due process and includes the obligation not to deny justice to foreign investors. Very importantly for our purposes, the existence of specific commitments may be decisive for the outcome of the investor's claim of breach of the FET standard. In particular, tribunals are likely to examine whether the state has made explicit or implicit promises to an investor, including that a legal and regulatory framework applicable to its investment would remain unchanged. Recent case law has stressed the role of specific commitments and representations made by the government to the investor. Where no such commitment has been made, the investor cannot expect the government to refrain from adopting new laws and policies.[49]

As the Tribunal noted in *Philip Morris v Uruguay*, if the argument that a host state must maintain a stable and predictable framework *consistent with the claimants' expectations* were to be upheld, then this would pave the way for other cases being filed against countries adopting tobacco control measures. Relying in part on the briefs that both the Pan American Health Organization (PAHO) and the WHO submitted in the case, the Tribunal rejected this view, in the absence of specific undertakings given by Uruguay to Philip Morris that it would not regulate tobacco:

---

[49] '[S]uch expectations would be neither legitimate nor reasonable': *EDF (Services) Ltd v Romania*, ICSID Case No. ARB/05/13, Award (2009), para 217.

429. ... The Claimants have provided no evidence of specific undertakings or representations made to them by Uruguay at the time of their investment (or, for that matter, subsequently). The present case concerns the formulation of general regulations for the protection of public health. There is no question of any specific commitment of the State or of any legitimate expectation of the Claimants vis-à-vis Uruguayan tobacco control regulations. Manufacturers and distributors of harmful products such as cigarettes can have no expectation that new and more onerous regulations will not be imposed, and certainly no commitments of any kind were given by Uruguay to the Claimants or (as far as the record shows) to anyone else.

430. On the contrary, in light of widely accepted articulations of international concern for the harmful effect of tobacco, the expectation could only have been of progressively more stringent regulation of the sale and use of tobacco products. Nor is it a valid objection to a regulation that it breaks new ground. Provisions such as Article 3(2) of the BIT do not preclude governments from enacting novel rules, even if these are in advance of international practice, provided these have some rational basis and are not discriminatory. Article 3(2) does not guarantee that nothing should be done by the host State for the first time.

It is interesting to note that the Tribunal specifically highlighted that the novelty of a measure was not a valid objection to its adoption, suggesting that IIL did not preclude governments from adopting groundbreaking regulations that had never been tested before, even if these were in advance of international practice. This is subject to the requirement that they are neither discriminatory nor arbitrary.

National regulators should also be particularly mindful of avoiding any significant inconsistencies in how policy measures are implemented and construed by various government departments and agencies at the national level. In effect, a legitimate expectations claim might be more likely to succeed if the investor exercised due diligence by seeking such a clarification and received a positive response, upon which it relied. This further highlights the importance for policy makers to secure cooperation from the outset between health experts, regulators, and lawyers to avoid such inconsistencies and maintain a coherent position throughout the policy process.[50]

Overall, therefore, the *Philip Morris v Uruguay* dispute confirms that governments are entitled to regulate to protect public health and that a changing regulatory environment can be part of their strategy. Importantly in this case, Uruguay had made no specific representations to Philip Morris that the law would not change, or that they would not be subject to stricter regulation. Moreover, the government's exercise of its regulatory powers was measured and reasonable: the Tribunal explicitly rejected the suggestion that it had acted arbitrarily. Had the government acted in an arbitrary manner or given specific representations to Philip Morris, it could well have found itself in a more difficult position.

8.5 The guarantee against uncompensated expropriation

Protecting foreign investors from *uncompensated* expropriation by a host state is another cornerstone of the IIL and such protection is also frequently invoked by investors in ISDS. Expropriation is the act of depriving an investor of the enjoyment of their investment.

The concept of expropriation is broadly construed, not only because of the broad definition of the very notion of investment, which – as was discussed earlier – potentially includes a wide range of assets from physical property and IP to contractual rights, but also because IIL protects investors

---

[50] A Mitchell and P O'Brien, 'If One Thai Bottle Should Accidentally Fall: Health Information, Alcohol Labelling and International Investment Law', *JWIT* 21 (2020) 674, at 690.

against both the direct taking of property and de facto or indirect expropriation. Indirect expropriation, which does not necessarily affect the legal title but rather its content, constitutes the typical form in which expropriations take place today.[51]

Article 5(1) of the BIT between Switzerland and Uruguay (1988)

Neither of the Contracting Parties shall take, either directly or indirectly, measures of expropriation, nationalization or any other measure having the same nature or the same effect against investments belonging to investors of the other Contracting Party, unless the measures are taken for the public benefit as established by law, on a non-discriminatory basis, and under due process of law, and provided that provisions be made for effective and adequate compensation. The amount of compensation, interest included, shall be settled in the currency of the country of origin of the investment and paid without delay to the person entitled thereto.

A host state imposing high taxes or regulatory requirements may undermine the ability of the investor to fully take advantage of its investment as anticipated and thereby make the foreign investment economically unviable, leading to challenges under IIL. For example, Philip Morris claimed that the adoption of tobacco standardization measures by Uruguay affected the 'meaningful use' of its IP rights and therefore constituted expropriation. As the Tribunal confirmed, it is nonetheless unlikely that a packaging standardization or other such NCD prevention measure amounts to expropriation:

In the Tribunal's view, in respect of a claim based on indirect expropriation, as long as sufficient value remains after the Challenged Measures are implemented, there

---

[51] For example, *Metalclad Corporation v The United Mexican States*, ICSID Case No. ARB(AF)/97/1.

is no expropriation. As confirmed by investment treaty decisions, a partial loss of the profits that the investment would have yielded absent the measure does not confer an expropriatory character on the measure.[52]

Following the adoption of Uruguay's contested measures, tobacco manufacturers have still been able to use their brands on their products. The same argument would hold for warning labels and marketing restrictions relating to alcohol and food. For example, producers subjected to a new legislation mandating front-of-pack warning labels and marketing restrictions could still use their trademarks on at least some of their products or reformulate those that do not meet the relevant thresholds.[53]

Very importantly, and following previous case law, the Tribunal in *Philip Morris v Uruguay* recalled that 'protecting public health has since long been recognised as an essential manifestation of the State's police power' and that 'the police powers doctrine has been applied in several cases to reject claims challenging regulatory measures designed specifically to protect public health'. However, to exclude any compensation, the host state must ensure that the measures: (i) have been taken bona fide; (ii) for the purposes of protecting public welfare; (iii) be non-discriminatory; and (iv) proportionate. It is therefore essential to distinguish simple regulatory measures from those which amount to indirect expropriation. It is worth highlighting here that these four factors refer to several principles discussed throughout this book.

A measure must be adopted *in good faith* and apply equally, *without discrimination against foreign investors* (as discussed earlier). In *Methanex*, which marked a clear shift in the assessment of the relationship between regulatory powers and

---

[52] *Philip Morris v Uruguay*, at para 286.
[53] M Campbell, 'NCD Prevention and International Investment Law in Latin America: Chile's Experience in Preventing Obesity and Unhealthy Diets', *JWIT* 21 (2020) 781.

alleged expropriation, the Tribunal ruled that the relevant environmental regulations adopted in California should have been foreseeable by the investor concluding that these regulations were a lawful regulation, not an expropriation.[54] The ban was implemented to protect the environment and the health of citizens, not to harm foreign investors, and California was motivated by an 'honest belief, held in good faith and on reasonable scientific grounds' that methanol contaminated ground water.[55] Similarly, in *Philip Morris v Uruguay*, the Tribunal emphasized the right of the state to fully and properly regulate matters of public health. It noted that 'protecting public health has long been recognized as an essential manifestation of the State's police power'. It also determined that 'whether a measure may be characterized as expropriatory depends on the nature and purpose of the State's action', before concluding that, in its view, there was not even a 'prima facie case of indirect expropriation of the 80/80 requirement'.[56]

A measure must also be proportionate and free from arbitrariness. This means that a rational relationship must exist between the measure adopted and the alleged purpose that the measure seeks to achieve,[57] and the impact of the measure on the investor must be proportional to the policy objective sought. There is some overlap in the nature of the inquiries made with respect to police powers and those relating to the 'arbitrariness' analysis for FET (see more on this later

---

[54] *Methanex v US* (2005), at para 15.

[55] *Methanex v US* (2005), at para 20. See also the subsequent *Chemtura* decision, at para 276. For a more detailed discussion of these two decisions, see further V Vadi, *Public Health in International Investment Law and Arbitration* (Abingdon: Routledge, 2012), pp 127–159.

[56] *Philip Morris v Uruguay*, at para 291.

[57] A Mitchell, 'Tobacco Plain Packaging Measures Affecting IP Protection under IIL: The Claims against Uruguay and Australia', in A Alemanno and E Bonadio, *Intellectual Property beyond Plain Packaging* (Cheltenham: Edward Elgar, 2016), p 213.

on). In practice, while the evaluation of proportionality and reasonableness can vary, arbitral tribunals have increasingly identified a 'margin of appreciation' to host states in designing their public policy measures. In *Philip Morris v Uruguay*, substantial discretion was granted in matters of public policy, particularly such 'acknowledged and major public health problems' as tobacco control. This case suggests that only measures that are 'entirely lacking in justification' or 'wholly disproportionate' will infringe IIL, as was discussed earlier.

Finally, the question arises whether an investor might also argue that the cumulative effect of the size of the warning combined with other aspects of the measure (for example, standardization of text and colours, or the chosen content of warnings), and the marketing rule (with its prohibition on the use of certain images and terms) further diminishes the value of the investment, tantamount to an expropriation. Tribunals accept that a state may engage in 'creeping expropriation',[58] over time, 'even though the State does not purport to have expropriated property and the legal title to that property formally remains with the original owner'.[59] Writing on the Chilean food labelling and marketing rules, Campbell has noted that the accumulated effects of the food labelling scheme and the advertising and marketing restrictions clearly represent a more intrusive interference with the rights and interests of foreign investors. However, Chile could argue that the degree of interference with foreign investments remains limited in scope; that the purpose of the measures is to protect public health in the context of a national obesity and NCDs epidemic; and that producers retain the possibility to reformulate their products to comply with the nutrient thresholds. This arguably

---

[58] For example, *Generation Ukraine v Ukraine*, Award, 16 September 2003.

[59] See C Giorgetti, 'Health and International Investment Law', in GL Burci and B Toebes, *Research Handbook in Global Health Law* (Cheltenham: Edward Elgar, 2018), Chapter 7.

rules out the existence of an indirect expropriation requiring compensation.[60]

8.6 Conclusions

Fundamentally, IIAs aim to promote regulatory environments promoting FDI, where foreign investors can operate in a stable environment without discrimination or other form of unfair treatment by host states. However, it can be used to challenge legitimate regulation that host states pursue in the public interest, including to protect public health and prevent NCDs. This is potentially problematic as IIAs are more intrusive than trade agreements. This is not only because FDI takes place within the borders of a state, but also because IIAs have gradually become regulating instruments that largely remain hidden from public scrutiny.[61] This may be particularly problematic since arbitration increases the power asymmetries that are associated with growing rates of NCDs worldwide.

Investors have a greater degree of control of an IIL dispute than a WTO dispute; in effect, investors choosing the WTO forum will have to rely upon their (or another) government's willingness to bring a claim. This is a prerogative and not an obligation for governments, which grants a significant margin of discretion to relevant policy makers. When potential violations of IP rights are limited in scope and discriminate against a foreign investor only, its home state may be reluctant

---

[60] M Campbell, 'Chile: Front-of-Package Warning Labels and Food Marketing', *Journal of Law, Medicine & Ethics* 50(2) (2022) 298; M Campbell, 'NCD Prevention and International Investment Law in Latin America: Chile's Experience in Preventing Obesity and Unhealthy Diets', *Journal of World Investment and Trade* 21 (2020) 781.

[61] Although IIAs are separate from the WTO and other trade agreements, investment commitments have been incorporated into some FTAs (for example, CPTPP), potentially bringing them into a more institutional framework that can support more transparent interactions between investors and governments.

to initiate a trade dispute because of political and *de minimis* considerations. Moreover, foreign investors are not always required to exhaust local remedies prior to engaging in ISDS. By consenting to international arbitration, states therefore delegate some portions of the judicial function to arbitrators, even regarding sensitive matters of public policy. One could speak of a paradigm shift vis-à-vis the traditional prerogative of the national judge. Finally, and crucially, the remedies available under IIL are different from those available in international trade law, with the possibility of significant financial compensation for investors, which unavoidably adds extra pressure on host states, particularly those with limited resources and capabilities.

Although IIAs can affect national policy making, there is a growing consensus that public health regulations that are evidence-based, carefully designed, non-discriminatory, consistently implemented, and appropriately targeted are less likely to be successfully contested under IIL. If contested, such measures are also more likely to withstand the challenge, provided that the measures are not arbitrary, and no specific representations have been made to investors encouraging a legitimate expectation that progressive regulation would not apply to them. On that basis, it is increasingly clear that governments have ample scope to regulate the tobacco, alcohol, and food industries to prevent NCDs, and even adopt novel, untested regulations, as the *Philip Morris v Uruguay* dispute has confirmed. However, states need to carefully exercise their discretion, bearing in mind that IIL case law dealing specifically with NCD prevention is still in its infancy. This cautious note is compounded by the fact that investment tribunals have not always been consistent in the absence of a doctrine of precedent in IIL, and that decisions are taken by a majority with the possibility of dissenting opinions.

The trajectory nonetheless suggests an increasingly refined approach to the relationship between public health and IIL, particularly as the doctrines of margin of appreciation and policy powers develop. This is not intended to suggest that tobacco, alcohol, and food MNCs will stop using IIL challenges as part of the gamut of lobbying strategies they use to delay and disrupt regulation. Nevertheless, building legal capacity and interdisciplinary strategic alliances will allow these challenges to be better anticipated and fought with poise and determination.

The fact that some portion of the iceberg remains hidden from view is a matter of significant concern, given the public policy implications of IIL disputes. This is particularly so as IIAs have shifted from being a protective 'shield' for defending corporations against unfair treatment to a 'sword' used by those same corporations to query legitimate government regulation in the public interest. This has given rise to a storm of criticism compounded by the fact that we have seen a dramatic increase of worldwide support for economic and social rights.[62] Therefore, beyond the evolution of IIL through judicial interpretation, some attempts have been made to rethink IIL more fundamentally.

In particular, many governments (including traditional capital-exporting states) have started to change their position on the desirability of ISDS. For example, Australia and New Zealand have, by mutual agreement, renounced the use of ISDS as between them under CPTPP.[63] This agreement is also particularly interesting for the important substantive carve-out it contains. Thus, even where governments still permit the use of investor arbitration between each other, tobacco control measures cannot be subject to ISDS.

We have also noted a move towards more balanced IIAs which contain 'right to regulate' clauses. Nevertheless, such clauses do not address the fundamental problem that such

---

[62] V Vadi, *Public Health in International Investment Law and Arbitration* (Abingdon: Routledge, 2012), p 64.

[63] Agreement between Australia and New Zealand Regarding Investor State Dispute Settlement, Trade Remedies and Transport Services (8 March 2018), by exchange of letters.

exception clauses do not place public policy measures on the same footing as investment protection standards; the entitlement of host states to pursue public policy objectives is framed as an exception, not a positive right. This is logical given the primary objectives pursued by IIL. In any event, if read in the light of broader state obligations, including their obligations under international human rights and global health law, these exceptions can and should be interpreted extensively.

Ultimately, and as Sattorova has argued, the potentially negative effect of IIAs on NCD prevention and public health more generally needs to be addressed not just through better regulatory flexibility provisions in the new and revised treaties but also through revisiting another tired and long-debated issue: the asymmetry of treaties as far as investor rights and obligations are concerned. To this effect, it is necessary to require that corporations act responsibly, beyond mere statements of corporate social responsibility. Priority should be on ensuring responsible investor behaviour through the incorporation into IIAs of provisions expressly addressing investor misconduct, such as bribery, corruption, and the exercise of improper influence over government officials).[64]

---

[64] M Sattorova, 'Investment Protection Agreements, Regulatory Chill, and National Measures On Childhood Obesity Prevention', in A Garde, J Curtis and O De Schutter, *Ending Childhood Obesity: A Challenge at the Crossroads of International Economic and Human Rights Law* (Cheltenham: Edward Elgar, 2020), 175–179.

NINE

Concluding Remarks

The purpose of this book has been to reflect on the relationship between international trade and investment law, on the one hand, and public health protection, on the other hand. Promoting a better understanding of this relationship, and therefore providing the tools required to build the legal capacity of public health and trade actors, is all the more important as tobacco, alcohol, and food MNCs seek to increase their presence in markets that are not as extensively regulated, not least in low- and middle-income countries. This, in turn, reinforces the need to introduce NCD interventions effectively and quickly across the globe. The more these MNCs utilize the opportunities that trade and investment liberalization offers, the more governments will need to ensure appropriate regulation of these MNCs, and, in turn, the more these MNCs will challenge such measures on international economic law grounds, and the more a solid grasp of international economic law will become paramount to prevent NCDs and promote better health for all around the world.

As we have noted throughout this book, challenges to governments take a variety of forms and are often combined. Importantly, they do not always present themselves only as formal legal challenges. These challenges from industry, often speaking through governmental actors, arise throughout the policy process. The structures of international economic law increase these 'entry points' for industry, not least through notification and other transparency commitments, which give industry additional notice that a measure is being prepared.

As economies and their supply chains have become more globalized and the rules underpinning them have developed (together with an elaborate institutional framework), legal arguments anchored in international economic law have been increasingly invoked to deter governments from regulating the tobacco, alcohol, and food industries to protect public health.

More specifically, legal challenges have included calls:

- to abandon or postpone governments' plans to regulate (for example, the introduction of tobacco plain packaging in New Zealand or Canada);
- to amend regulation to better suit industry interests:
  - in the *personal* scope of protection such as lowering the age of the protected child from 18 to 14 (for example, Chilean food marketing restrictions) or from 18 to 16 (as in Portugal); or
  - in the *material* scope of protection, such as insisting on exemptions of certain economic sectors (for example, the UK exemption of milk-based beverages from the sugar industry levy), or by insisting on different labelling formats (for example, FoPNL in Latin American countries), or different health warnings (for example, on alcoholic beverages in Thailand or on tobacco products all over the world); or
- to delay implementation (for example, the delay to the implementation of both the placement and price promotion and the marketing restrictions on unhealthy food in the UK, or the delay to the implementation of Scotland's alcohol minimum unit pricing legislation).

At times, the tobacco, alcohol, and food industries have challenged governments directly, most notably as parties to international investment law disputes, as was the case in *Philip Morris v Uruguay*. These direct challenges are only the tip of the iceberg: often, these industry actors also challenge governments indirectly when calling upon or assisting governments interested in protecting the interests of exporting industries. This happens both in formal trade disputes (for example, *US – Clove Cigarettes* and *Australia – Tobacco Plain Packaging* at the WTO) and in diplomatic forums (for example, when raising specific trade concerns at the TBT Committee against FoPNL, alcohol health warnings, or other public health interventions). International trade and investment law arguments may also be raised before national or regional courts.

International trade and investment law has been in the public eye and used extensively by economic actors, and tobacco, alcohol, and food MNCs more specifically, to challenge national regulation that affect their short-term economic interests. This does not mean that other bodies of international law are not important too; aside for their own *direct* impact, they can also contribute to interpretation of other bodies of rules, as the use of the FCTC in tobacco-related trade and investment disputes has demonstrated.

Throughout this book, we have been clear that while international economic law was never intended to *protect* public health per se, it was not designed to harm it either. Neither international trade law nor international investment law prevents governments from exercising their discretion to regulate trade and investment with a view to achieving public health objectives. As we have shown, governments have ample leeway to regulate the tobacco, alcohol, and food industries to prevent NCDs both in the *extent* to which they seek to protect health on their territory and in the *means* they deploy to this effect. Both international trade law and international investment law grant them a broad margin of discretion to protect legitimate public interest objectives, and public health more specifically. The case law in these areas of law has evolved over the past two decades to address complex health issues, including the prevention of NCDs. As a result, the view has become more firmly established that governments can adopt the wide range of measures required to effectively prevent NCDs, while being compliant with their international economic law obligations. Some of these measures will be the first of their kind, as was the case with tobacco plain packaging. Others may well take inspiration from others, as the development of FoPNL in Latin America demonstrates. Both the international trade and investment law regimes allow for a degree of experimentation on the part of governments, even if this means imposing legal obligations that industry actors forcefully oppose. The challenge is not that the law presents insurmountable difficulties for governments; rather, it is that *accounts* of what the law requires from certain industry actors may. We hope that this book contributes to correcting that misconception.

Additionally, it is not only that governments *may* act to prevent NCDs, but that in many instances they are under an *obligation* to do so in order to meet their international human rights and global health obligations. The reconciliation of distinct bodies of international law is not only possible but also desirable, as the use of the FCTC in tobacco control disputes both at the WTO and in arbitration proceedings illustrates.[1] 'If law successfully manages conflicts, then repeated conflicts should actually strengthen the legal order.'[2]

---

[1] J Curtis and A Garde, 'Overcoming the legal challenge to end childhood obesity: Pathways towards positive harmonization in law and Governance', in A Garde et al (eds), *Ending Childhood Obesity: A Challenge at the Crossroads of International Economic and Human Rights Law* (Cheltenham: Edward Elgar, 2020), pp 339–370.

[2] V Vadi, *Public Health in International Investment Law and Arbitration* (Abingdon: Routledge, 2012), p 175, quoting Pauwelyn.

Nevertheless, when exercising their regulatory powers to prevent NCDs through the adoption of population-wide measures intended to limit the consumption of tobacco, alcohol, and unhealthy food, governments must act within the parameters set by international economic law. WTO law, IIAs, and FTAs are legally binding on their parties. They are not mere declarations of intent. Moreover, these legally binding obligations are even more likely to 'bite' as they are accompanied by dispute settlement mechanisms that ensure a level of compliance that few other bodies of international law can achieve.

One could envisage international trade law and investment law as rules for traffic: they are restrictions that limit how one can go about one's business, while still permitting destinations to be reached.[3] The Appellate Body has been explicit about this, stating that 'it is within the authority of a WTO Member to set the public health or environmental objectives it seeks to achieve, as well as the level of protection that it wants to obtain, through the measure or the policy it chooses to adopt'.[4] This does not underestimate the challenge of dealing with highly complex policy challenges such as NCD prevention – a situation also explicitly acknowledged by the Appellate Body, that 'certain complex public health or environmental problems may be tackled only with a comprehensive policy comprising a multiplicity of interacting measures'.[5]

---

[3] G Messenger, 'Sugar as Commodity or Health Risk: The Unmaking or Remaking of International Trade Law?', in A Garde, J Curtis, and O de Schutter, *Ending Childhood Obesity: A Challenge at the Crossroads of International Economic and Human Rights Law* (Cheltenham: Edward Elgar, 2020), pp 112–137.

[4] Appellate Body Report, *Brazil – Measures Affecting Imports of Retreaded Tyres*, WT/DS322/AB/R (3 December 2007), para 140 (footnotes omitted).

[5] Appellate Body Report, *Brazil – Measures Affecting Imports of Retreaded Tyres*, WT/DS322/AB/R (3 December 2007), para 151.

Table 9.1: Principles and government best practice

Predictability	Governments must be open about what they do and prepare to engage with the trade community to reflect on the underpinning justification for the proposed measures. This will include trading partners in the context of the WTO and FTAs and foreign investors in the context of international investment law. Ensuring that businesses have been put on notice and given appropriate (that is, not overly long) time to prepare or adjust can support compliance with this principle.
Non-discrimination	Whether in relation to trading partners or foreign investors, governments need to ensure that products or investors from abroad are not discriminated against in a way that cannot be justified on the basis of a legitimate policy objective. Non-discrimination is a cornerstone of international economic law. Businesses will be quick to identify (and challenge) discriminatory measures.
Necessity	Governments need to ensure that the measures they take pursue legitimate policy objectives, are suitable to achieve the objectives pursued, and take account of the imperative of balancing competing interests. This requires that measures be justified and anchored in an appropriately rigorous evidence base, acknowledging that reasoned and justified policy experimentation is permissible. Reflecting on the relationship between the specific objectives pursued and the means deployed to achieve these objectives is paramount.
Consistency	Where possible, aligning with international approaches, whether through applying international standards such as those developed by the Codex Alimentarius Commission, or through applying the WHO FCTC and WHO guidelines or policy recommendations, or through applying best practice, to ensure consistent and reasonable policy making, plays an important role in being able to defend measures which may have trade, investment, or IP implications.

Our analysis has identified key principles that should underpin the policy process and the creation, adoption, and implementation of new NCD prevention measures. The goal should never be to successfully defend a measure in litigation, but, rather, to do one's utmost to ensure that it never reaches that stage. Alignment with the principles discussed throughout this book should go a long way towards supporting this aim and, in instances of threatened litigation, provides a stronger foundation to successfully defend challenges to evidence-based NCD prevention laws and policies.

Although the international trade and investment law regimes are not principally focused on protecting public health in a narrow sense, tools of trade and investment policy can be. And in aligning the desire to leverage the powerful tools at governments' disposal (including taxes, tariffs, packaging or labelling requirements, claims regulation, and many others with existing commitments), it is important to have a clear sense of how these policy tools should be developed from an international economic law perspective.

Public health has always been a cornerstone of state sovereignty. It has now also become an emerging field of international law. In parallel, international trade and investment law have developed and become more sophisticated to respond to public health concerns. As Vadi has noted, the interaction between these two fields of law may be seen as complementary as public health is a core component of poverty reduction, human development, and economic growth, while trade liberalization and FDI are intended to promote development.[6] There may be a positive synergy. Ultimately: 'The increasing relevance of public health in international law discourse can have a positive influence on humanizing international economic relations.'[7]

---

[6] The success or otherwise of liberalization as pursued to date to support development is, of course, contentious.

[7] V Vadi, *Public Health in International Investment Law and Arbitration* (Abingdon: Routledge, 2012), p 193.

We have seen the influence that industry actors play, often working against governments seeking to develop NCD prevention policies, in multiple different countries, courts, and institutions. And while debate is ongoing about the effectiveness or desirability of these different legal regimes, it is important to stress that NCD prevention measures *can* be developed by governments under the existing system.

Legal challenges (and indeed the threat of them) are potentially costly for governments, irrespective of their outcomes, as the costs incurred by Uruguay and by Australia in defending the challenges mounted against their tobacco packaging measures demonstrate. Moreover, beyond formal litigation costs, there is a significant cost related to the amount of time and resource that governments spend on addressing these challenges, whether in their own ministries or through overseas embassies or trade missions. Nevertheless, where governments anticipate these disputes, from design to implementation, and defend them effectively from both formal and informal challenges, such disputes can constitute major victories for public health and lay the groundwork for other governments envisaging similar measures. In this sense, the wider international community benefits from each successfully introduced measure, as the rapid spread over the past decade of both tobacco plain packaging and FoPNL legislation has demonstrated, however pioneering such measures may be.

The best defence to such challenges is knowledge:

- knowledge of the international trade and investment law commitments that governments have made and must therefore uphold as NCD prevention laws and policies are developed, adopted, and implemented;
- knowledge of the strength of a government's evidence base and therefore its legal position; and
- knowledge of how it can best frame such evidence in light of its international trade and investment law commitments to be in a stronger position to convince the international

community of the legitimacy of the NCD prevention laws and policies under review.

The lack of political will to tackle NCDs has been linked to two main factors: the power asymmetries stemming from the power (economic and political) of major tobacco, alcohol, and food MNCs; and the lack of implementation research demonstrating what can and cannot work.[8] We hope that, in a small way, this book has contributed to reflecting on both these aspects, and thereby to the knowledge base required to address challenges to NCD prevention measures, notably those anchored in international trade and investment law.

[8] G Loffreda, S Arekelyan, I Bou-Orm, H Holmer, LN Allen, S Witter, et al, 'Barriers and opportunities for WHO "best buys" non-communicable disease policy adoption and implementation from a political economy perspective: A complexity systematic review', *International Journal of Health Policy and Management* 13 (2024) 7989.

Selected Bibliography

We have purposefully been very selective in the choice of references we have listed here. Our aim was first and foremost to provide key monographs, reports, and edited collections dealing specifically with international economic law (both trade and investment law), public health law and non-communicable diseases (NCD) prevention, or international economic law and NCD prevention. This selection is not intended to suggest that other references are not helpful in understanding these fields of law and how they interact. We have mentioned several of them in the footnotes, although – here again – we have purposefully been selective.

Trade law and policy

The WTO website is an excellent resource for introductory information as well as more detailed information about the policies and activities of governments. See in particular:

- WTO, 'Understanding the WTO': https://www.wto.org/engl ish/thewto_e/whatis_e/tif_e/tif_e.htm
- WTO, 'Trade Policy Reviews' (for information on specific WTO Members' trade policies): https://www.wto.org/english/tratop_ e/tpr_e/tpr_e.htm
- WTO, 'Analytical Index' (for legal analysis of specific provisions of WTO agreements): https://www.wto.org/english/res_e/pub lications_e/ai17_e/ai17_e.htm

The following are a selection of introductory books and textbooks on the detail of international trade law (principally WTO law):

- H Gao, J Hillman, N Lamp and J Pauwelyn, *The International Trade Law Casebook*: https://genevatradeplatform.org/e-casebook/
- P van den Bossche and D Prévost, *Essentials of WTO Law* (Cambridge: Cambridge University Press, 2nd edn, 2021)
- P van den Bossche and W Zdouc, *The Law and Policy of the World Trade Organization: Text, Cases and Materials* (Cambridge: Cambridge University Press, 5th edn, 2021)
- S Lester, B Mercurio and A Davies, *World Trade Law: Text, Materials and Commentary* (Oxford: Hart Publishing, 3rd edn, 2022)

For a detailed historical and legal analysis of all WTO legal provisions:

- P-T Stoll and H Hestermeyer, *Commentaries on World Trade Law* (Leiden: Brill, 2nd edn, 2022)

Useful entries on the policy context of trade relations include:

- A Narlikar, *The World Trade Organization: A Very Short Introduction* (Oxford: Oxford University Press, 2005)
- LL Martin, *The Oxford Handbook of the Political Economy of International Trade* (Oxford: Oxford University Press, 2015)

The following texts provide a useful overview on the ways in which trade law and public health can interact:

- C Button, *The Power to Protect: Trade, Health and Uncertainty in the WTO* (Oxford: Hart Publishing, 2004)
- G Bermann and P Mavroidis (eds), *Trade and Human Health and Safety* (Cambridge: Cambridge University Press, 2006)
- B McGrady, *Trade and Public Health: The WTO, Tobacco, Alcohol, and Diet* (Cambridge: Cambridge University Press, 2011)

- G van Calster and D Prévost (eds), *Research Handbook on Environment, Health and the WTO* (Cheltenham: Edward Elgar, 2013)
- D Gleeson and R Labonté, *Trade Agreements and Public Health: A Primer for Health Policy Makers, Researchers and Advocates* (London: Palgrave Macmillan, 2020)

On IP in WTO law, see:

- M Kennedy, *WTO Dispute Settlement and the Trips Agreement: Applying Intellectual Property Standards in a Trade Law Framework* (Cambridge: Cambridge University Press, 2018)
- A Taubman, H Wager and J Watal, *A Handbook on the WTO TRIPS Agreement* (Cambridge: Cambridge University Press, 2nd edn, 2020)
- CM Correa, *Trade Related Aspects of Intellectual Property Rights: A Commentary on the TRIPS Agreement* (Oxford: Oxford University Press, 2nd edn, 2020)

On TRIPS, IP and NCDs more specifically, see:

- WTO, 'Guide to the TRIPS Agreement': https://www.wto.org/english/tratop_e/trips_e/ta_modules_e.htm
- A Alemanno and E Bonadio, *Intellectual Property beyond Plain Packaging* (Cheltenham: Edward Elgar, 2016)

Investment law and policy

UN Trade and Development (UNCTAD) provides an excellent selection of resources for those interested in investment issues, including a comprehensive database of international investment agreements. See:

- UNCTAD, 'Investment Policy Hub': https://investmentpolicy.unctad.org/
- UNCTAD, 'International Investment Agreement Navigator': https://investmentpolicy.unctad.org/international-investment-agreements

The following books provide an overview of the content of international investment law:

- J Bonnitcha, LN Skovgaard Poulsen, and M Waibel, *The Political Economy of the Investment Treaty Regime* (Oxford: Oxford University Press, 2017)
- M Sattorova, *The Impact of Investment Law on Host States* (Oxford: Hart Publishing, 2018)
- K Nadakvukaren Schefer, *International Investment Law: Text, Cases and Materials* (Cheltenham: Edward Elgar, 3rd edn, 2020)
- A Reinisch, *Advanced Introduction to International Investment Law* (Cheltenham: Edward Elgar, 2020)
- M Sornarajah, *The International Law on Foreign Investment* (Cambridge: Cambridge University Press, 5th edn, 2021)
- R Dolzer, U Kriebaum, and C Schreuer, *Principles of International Investment Law* (Oxford: Oxford University Press, 3rd edn, 2022)
- D Collins, *An Introduction to International Investment Law* (Cambridge: Cambridge University Press, 2023)

On the relationship between investment law, public health and NCD prevention more specifically, see:

- V Vadi, *Public Health in International Investment Law and Arbitration* (Abingdon: Routledge, 2013)
- A Garde and J Zrilic (eds), 'Non-Communicable Diseases Prevention and International Investment Law', Special Issue of the *Journal of World Investment and Trade*, 21 (2020) 649

For other references addressing the relationship between public health, NCDs, and law:

- A Garde, *EU Law and Obesity Prevention* (Dordrecht: Kluwer, 2010)
- G Howells, *The Tobacco Challenge* (Abingdon: Routledge, 2011)
- A Mitchell and T Voon, *The Global Tobacco Epidemic and the Law* (Cheltenham: Edward Elgar, 2011)

- A Mitchell, T Voon, and J Liberman (eds), *Public Health and Plain Packaging of Cigarettes: Legal Issues* (Cheltenham: Edward Elgar, 2012)
- A Alemanno and A Garde (eds), *Regulating Lifestyle Risks* (Cambridge: Cambridge University Press, 2014)
- T Voon, A Mitchell, and J Liberman (eds), Regulating Tobacco, Alcohol and Unhealthy Foods: The Legal Issues (Abingdon: Routledge, 2015)
- G Burci and B Toebes (eds), *Research Handbook on Global Health Law* (Cheltenham: Edward Elgar, 2018)
- L Gruszcynski, *The Regulation of E-Cigarettes* (Cheltenham: Edward Elgar, 2019)
- M Elske Gipsen and B Toebes, *Human Rights and Tobacco Control* (Cheltenham: Edward Elgar, 2020)
- A Garde, J Curtis and O De Schutter (eds), *Ending Childhood Obesity: A Challenge at the Crossroads of International Economic and Human Rights Law* (Cheltenham: Edward Elgar, 2020)
- M Melillo, *Weaponising Evidence: A History of Tobacco Control in International Law* (Cambridge: Cambridge University Press, 2024)

Index

References to figures appear in *italic* type; those in **bold** type refer to tables. References to footnotes show both the page number and the note number (98n3).

www.ingramcontent.com/pod-product-compliance
Lightning Source LLC
Chambersburg PA
CBHW071602210326
41597CB00019B/3368